MISSION FIRST
PEOPLE ALWAYS

MISSION FIRST
PEOPLE ALWAYS

By Mike Patterson, Ed.D.

Foreword by Gil Brady, Ed.D.

ISBN: 978-0-578-93675-8

What proven leaders are saying about *Mission First, People Always*

"Calling Mission First, People Always a great book on leadership would be accurate, but it would fail to recognize that it is also a great book about learning. And calling it a book about the people side of the business would fall short of acknowledging that it is also a book about performance. And calling Michael Patterson an exemplary thinker and writer would neglect to recognize his superior storytelling skills. In this one must-read book, Patterson artfully shares perspectives that every leader and aspiring leader should read."

- Mark Allen, Ph.D.

Pepperdine University Professor and Chair, Master of Science in Human Resources Program and author, *The Corporate University Handbook* and *Aha Moments in Talent Management*.

"Dr. Mike Patterson has proved to be a deeply trusted and competent advisor on complex topics. Not only do you get a depth of expertise when working with Mike, but you get someone with great heart, who is truly passionate about his work. For leaders at all levels, this book will quickly become a permanent resident on your bedside table."

- Andy Harrison

Senior Director, Leadership Development, McKesson

"The fire service is long known for its unwavering commitment to service. *Mission First, People Always* provides a roadmap for purpose-driven leaders who want to remain focused on the mission, while caring for the people around them and building healthy organizations. I recommend it for leaders who care enough to make a difference."

-Ivan Rojer

Fire Chief, Southern California

"*Mission First, People Always* combines practical experience, academic research, and unique stories to inspire the kind of leadership we need to build stronger, more productive, and more human-centered organizations. A fantastic read for those beginning a leadership journey and for those who need to reset."

-Ludmila N. Praslova, Ph.D., SHRM-SCP

Professor and Director of Research, Graduate Organizational Psychology, Vanguard University of Southern California

"...the perfect book for leaders who are looking for strategies to maintain the right balance between meeting the mission and taking care of people. As a 30-year military and federal government leader, it is very clear that Mike has captured the key elements that an effective leader needs to thrive in any environment and succeed. These are the same principles that the men and women of the White House Communications Agency employ every day to every mission. I cannot wait to provide copies to my mentees and coaching clients who are on a leadership journey and looking for tools that will make them the best leader that they can be."

-Darrell Williams
CEO, Alliance Seminars Coaching & White House Communications Agency Hall of Fame Inductee

"For those in relentless pursuit of growth in daily leadership practices, Mike's book is a thought-provoking guide to the artful balance of performance and people. Emerging and experienced leaders will be reminded that it isn't about the answers so much as continually asking the right questions."

-Commissioner Judy Fitzgerald
Georgia Department of Behavioral Health and Developmental Disabilities

"There are certain foundational skills young leaders must develop and seasoned leaders must maintain. Mission First, People Always teaches these essential lessons with a delightful blend of theory, practice, and engaging stories. Each chapter offers tremendous value, so a busy leader can benefit from just a few minutes reading, reflecting, and then applying the clearly presented message. Rarely do I come across a leadership book that serves a wide audience, but the Mission First, People Always perspective is something every leader needs."

-Kathy Barham
Director, Global Learning and Development, Abbott Diagnostics

"Mike hits a home run in addressing the tension that is felt when leading any organization. This timely book is a must read for new leaders and experienced leaders alike."

-Dr. Bruce K. Terpstra
President of Consentia Group

"Inspiring, provocative, and refreshing. Mike Patterson's depth of experience with leadership topics is made warmly accessible through his genuine passion for people. Reading Mike is like sitting down with a close colleague whose words and wisdom are far more valuable than any discomfort they may necessitate."

-Peter Gleason, Ph.D.
Associate Professor of Psychology, Thomas College

"I am privileged to know Dr. Mike Patterson as both a friend and as a highly respected leader who has supported the training of our entire church denomination in the principles described in this new work, Mission First; People Always. What a joy it is to say that Mike walks the talk! He is about both mission and people and highly effective in both areas. I've been privileged to see Mike train both very large rooms of high-level business executives, and a handful of young leaders starting a new church, as a kind gesture to them and to me. He was equally passionate and impactful, as well as kind and gracious in both environments. I have no doubt that all who read this book will become better leaders."

-Rev. David Reynolds
Western Church Planting Alliance

"If you desire to lead, or are a new leader, grab this book! If you are a veteran leader, grab this book! You will be challenged to hone your craft while ensuring success for the mission and your people."

-Stephen E. Childs
Chief Experience Officer, Farm Credit Mid-America

"Leaders are often advised to reflect on their leadership, but many don't know where to start. This book guides leaders into the introspective reflection necessary for exemplary leadership."

-Jeannette Guignard, Ed.D.
Organizational Leadership Professor, California Baptist University

"For mission-centered people like me, this is a handbook to help us achieve balance. Loaded with tips and practical exercises, it is a book you will want to highlight, tab, and refer back to several times a year!"

-George "Bud" Baker, Ed.D.
CAPT, USN (Ret.)

"Loved it! Easy to read yet profound in its insights. The sections at the end of each chapter provide realistic and workable ways to apply the material. A must read for every team that values its members and wants to move forward with meaningful success."

-Dr. Larry G. Shelton
founder of Soulmates For Life

"Mission First, People Always is a must read packed with purposeful and practical guidance for those who know that lifelong learning impacts results and relationships equally. By embracing Dr. Mike's coaching, you will quickly find yourself building the muscle needed to consistently meet the needs of people while fearlessly pursuing big goals."

-Kim Kerr
Team & Organizational Consultant, BASF Global Business Services

"Crafting a balance between people and performance is paramount in this age of disruption. Like other K-12 Districts around the world, Houston ISD had to pivot very quickly to provide equity, access, and inclusion for all. Dr. Patterson's newest book, *Mission First, People Always*, is a reminder of our 'why' and how to reinvest in our commitment. The mission first and foremost is to educate the whole child, but this must be coupled with care for our students and teachers. We must do both.

This book, in the hands of my team, will be a tool to build a culture that fulfills the mission and keeps teachers, students, and the community first!"

-Dana Carmouche, MBA
Sr. Manager, Career Readiness, Houston Independent School District

To all of the purpose-driven leaders I have encountered over the years who have served the people around them and their organization's mission with equal fervor: Your balanced approach has shaped me and continues to inspire me.

"Love and truth form a good leader; sound leadership is founded on loving integrity."

Proverbs 20:28 (The Message)

foreword

THERE IS NO recipe or formula for integrating concern for people and commitment to the mission at hand. As a young man, I believed that I would someday find that delicate balance. I can honestly say my friendship with the author has greatly helped me explore this matter more productively and creatively.

Mike and I met in the early days of our careers. We have a fair amount in common, including that we both served in the military and later were fortunate to work for TAP Pharmaceuticals. Mike and I served as first-line managers, and although we only worked together for a short time, I remember thinking that we were quite alike in some ways but very different in others.

Thankfully, our worlds continued to intersect even after I left TAP. My doctoral studies led to an interest in finding a way to assess people's personalities and how they change in the face of conflict. A friend suggested that I contact someone we had both worked with in the past. Fortunately, this turned out to be Dr. Mike Patterson, who introduced me to an assessment called the Strength Deployment Inventory (SDI).

The SDI certification process did not disappoint. Learning more about relationship awareness theory (the academic underpinning of the SDI assessment), as well as the importance of assessing motive in good times and in conflict, produced a sense that I was leaning into a deeper understanding of myself as a leader. I was developing a new perspective on the connection between leaders and the way in which leadership emerges on truly great teams.

This started a new phase in my friendship with Dr. Patterson. Mike was working on his first book, *Have a Nice Conflict,* and I was launching my consulting company, Relationship Impact. As we found ourselves working together more and more, and I learned about the manner in which people prioritize motives, it was becoming more apparent why I had detected a "difference" between us. In short, Mike's primary motive is performance and mine is people. Or, as he has so expertly explored in this book, Mike tends to focus on the mission, while my focus leans toward relationships.

My relationship and my friendship with Dr. Patterson have grown over the past 10 years, and so has my respect for him and admiration for his work. Mike is uniquely qualified to write this book, and I am extremely grateful he has taken the time to share his perspective on the challenge of integrating mission accomplishment and concern for people. I have witnessed Mike work with organizations to explore how best to balance these two priorities. More importantly, I have watched him live out these lessons in his personal life.

Perhaps the most compelling aspect of our friendship is how often we have had completely different perspectives on situations that involved both of us. Yet, over our years of working together – often during really stressful times – we have come to realize how much better we both are because we can learn from each other constantly.

Mike has worked incredibly hard to embrace his performance-oriented perspective while recognizing those moments he may be likely to overstep. I have done the same with my people-oriented perspective. I feel fortunate to say that I am a better leader today because Mike has truly helped me navigate those moments when a mission-first viewpoint was needed. And I like to think I have provided similar assistance to him in people-first situations.

This dynamic can best be understood through a story set a few years ago. I was working on my dissertation and had asked Dr. Patterson to join my committee as a reader because I knew he would challenge me to do truly meaningful work. I also knew Mike was an outstanding leadership scholar and that I would learn a great deal from him.

About two years into the undertaking, I had completed my research and was composing the final write-up for my committee to review. And I was stuck. It seemed that each time I read the paper, I would find another section that needed to be reworked, rewritten, and reorganized.

My committee was growing impatient, and I was going a bit mad. I was focused on trying to think about each committee member and ensuring that my work addressed each of their interests and each of their previously expressed concerns or helpful feedback. So, I did what I often do when the mission or goal seemed to be slipping away. I called Mike.

Mike did two things. First, he listened. As I spoke through my various concerns and went through the even greater number of paths I had identified in terms of moving forward, he listened. He asked excellent questions and allowed me to express my concerns in terms of writing a dissertation considerate of each of the committee members. People always.

Then, he did this: He told me, "Gil, it's time to send your dissertation to the committee".

I protested, again explaining the various parts of the paper I felt were not developed enough and perhaps unclear. Again, Mike listened.

Then, he said again, "Turn it in."

And I did. Mission first.

As Mike had predicted, the committee reacted very positively to the paper. They also had many comments, suggestions, and questions for me. The number was much less than I expected, and their positive impact on my work was immense.

Leading and learning are iterative. So is life. This book is essential for anyone who cares about leading effectively – in such a way that team members look back with pride and gratitude for having been a meaningful part of the effort. Leading in such a way that challenging goals are met while people also find themselves growing, learning, and preparing for more responsibility in the future. Leading in a way that truly makes a difference and makes people's lives better.

Dr. Patterson is an excellent guide. He is committed to making sure that reading this book is a wise investment of time. Mike gets things done and, therefore, hates to waste people's time. This book honors the reader's time by providing practical and executable strategies for balancing the mission and the care of the people pursuing it.

Dr. Patterson deeply wants each person who reads this book to learn something meaningful about themselves and about the people they are privileged to lead. Readers will discover an insight about who they want to be and who others perceive them to be that will improve their leadership skills and results.

I am grateful for having had the opportunity to explore this dynamic with Mike of balancing mission and people. He is a great role model, and everything he writes in this book, he practices himself. I have seen it.

And I am a better leader because of it.

— Gil Brady, Ed.D.

Table of Contents

foreword xi

introduction 3

1 getting started
what's it like to be on the other end of you? 11

2 what's the mission?
the north star that provides direction 19

3 why does the mission matter?
how to create a culture of commitment 41

4 who is on your island?
the power of collaboration 61

5 words matter
so choose them carefully 79

6 please, disagree
healthy teams have healthy opposition 105

7 the conflict chronicles
how to change the story 133

8 people are always watching
what do they see? 155

9 keep looking for the pony
the virtuous cycle that creates relationship 175

10 the one thing
it all comes down to relationships 199

appendix 211

acknowledgements 217

about the author 220

introduction

EVERY NOW AND then, we encounter leadership so compelling that we stop what we're doing, take notice, and then are overwhelmingly grateful for those who excel when the stakes are sky high and the odds against them even higher. This was the case the day a billion people paused to applaud Luis Urzua.

Nothing seemed unusual on Aug. 5, 2010, as Mr. Urzua began his shift as a foreman at the gold and copper mine in San Jose, Chili. But in the blink of an eye, everything changed. The mine collapsed under a rock the size of the Empire State Building, trapping Urzua and his crew of 32 miners in a subterranean prison for the next 69 days.

Emergency provisions were designed to last only 48 hours, and with little hope of immediate rescue, Urzua's first priority was to keep his men alive. The first few hours were chaotic, as dust filled the air, concealing the true extent of the damage. When the dust finally settled, Urzua knew the wait for help would be a long one.

During the first 17 days – when the group had no contact with the outside world – Urzua allowed the men only small sips of milk and bites of tuna every other day.[1] Later, when they could communicate with rescue workers above ground, he boldly advocated for his

---

1   Wil Longbottom, "Last man standing: The foreman who refused to give up and remained 2,000 ft down until all his men were safe," DailyMail.com, October 14, 2010, available at https://www.dailymail.co.uk/news/article-1320371/CHILEAN-MINERS-RESCUE-Luis-Urzua-foreman-refused-up.html (Accessed January 2021).

crew with Sebastian Pinera, Chile's president, pleading that they not be forgotten and that every effort be made to free them.

Countries around the world responded by sending experts and resources to help bring the trapped miners home. At last, rescuers were able to lower the aptly named Phoenix escape vehicle to the trapped men, who climbed aboard the cramped capsule one by one. It took several hours to ferry all of them to the surface, but as each man emerged, the waiting crowd went wild. Like any good captain, the last man out was Urzua, who was greeted by the Chilean president under a banner that read, "Mission Accomplished."

The media rightly hailed Luis Urzua as a hero. However, before the collapse, he was a simple shift foreman known by relatively few people. The transformation from status quo to hero occurred as he balanced the human needs of his crew with the overarching mission: their survival and escape. This is the essential call of leadership – the ability to balance task accomplishment and relationship.

In a world deeply scarred by a global pandemic, racial injustice, corruption, violence, fires, economic headwinds, and the continued threat of terrorism, we need leaders now more than ever. But then, we have always needed leaders. In our darkest moments, we look to them to get us to the other side. We expect our leaders to provide encouragement and direction in the face of doubt and confusion. We ask them to see around corners, find opportunities, and help us win. Leaders matter and we expect a lot from them.

We ask so much from them, they probably should have superpowers. Of course, none do. Some disappoint in the end, while many get the job done in a lackluster way. A few, however, become extraordinary. Surprisingly, perhaps, relatively few receive formal leadership training before beginning their journey. Most leadership skills are learned on the job, but truth be told, some leaders give little thought to how they are leading.

Some have direct reports and an auspicious title that makes their status and authority quite clear. Others routinely practice leadership – some with great skill – but have no direct reports, fancy title, or formal authority. They influence, guide, and get things done because that's what is needed in the situation. Thank goodness for these emergent leaders, even though many do not see themselves that way.

This reality compels us to broaden our view and definition of leaders and leadership. That's a tall task, though. Author Jacob Morgan asked 140 CEOs of top, world-class organizations to define leadership and got 140 different responses![2] Even these senior executives, collectively responsible for the lives of millions of people, could not come close to agreeing on a single definition.

Every definition of leadership tends to revolve around the central themes of people and performance.

All address the necessity of getting something done, accomplishing a mission, or achieving a goal, and doing it always involves people.

---

2 Jacob Morgan, *The Future Leader: 9 Skills and Mindsets to Succeed in the Next Decade*, First Edition. Hoboken, NJ: John Wiley & Sons, 2020, pp. 17-19.

Both elements are essential for any sort of work or organization – at least that's the foundational premise on which everything in this book is based.

Of course, this isn't a new idea. I was first exposed to this philosophy of leadership as a young U.S. Army officer. "Mission first, people always" was a mantra in my leadership training and an oft-repeated refrain in every unit in which I served. The other military branches embrace the same idea, probably because it's a wonderfully concise way of emphasizing the two inseparable aspects of leadership.

Unfortunately, catchy as it may be, the statement can also be nebulous and even cliché. It may look good on a poster, but it doesn't provide useful guidance for the folks in the trenches. No one really knows what it means, much less how to do it consistently. My goal in writing this book is to see a platitude become daily practice by inviting leaders to think deeply about what it means to get things done – within their personal context.

Who Should Read this Book?

Fledgling leaders will find this book to be a crash course in the everyday essentials for success. It's also a primer of sorts for laying a firm foundation on which to build a long-range personal development plan. Think of it like the lower levels of a scaffold. You'll need a strong base before you climb higher and develop a personal philosophy of leadership that guides you through complex challenges. But no matter how far you go on your leadership journey, you have to begin with the essentials.

For more seasoned leaders, the words on these pages present an opportunity to reconsider key concepts through the lens of experience. In some cases, you'll replay situations in your mind and examine past actions. Don't second-guess yourself, or the decisions of others; however, your personal history will provide a means to contextualize abstract ideas and bring them to life – your life. Reflection questions at the end of each chapter encourage you to apply these concepts.

Some readers have been on the leadership journey for many years, and now it's legacy time. Preparing the next generation of leaders is the top priority, and you're looking for a framework on which you can hang your personal experiences and lessons learned as you coach and mentor others. Feel free to add your own "war stories" to help make some of my points. People tend to remember a good story.

Still others will pick up this book because they are responsible for leadership development for their team or organization. In that case, you have undoubtedly recognized the magnitude of this challenge – leadership is a very broad topic and there's a lot of material out there to consider. More importantly, your initiatives must be shaped to the culture, constraints, and needs of your organization, and that's **always** a tall order.

Fortunately, this book helps with that, as well. You will find that each chapter, with its reflection questions and action items, can be the basis for a lesson or portion of your curriculum that you can build out and customize for your organization. I'll even suggest additional reading and resources to help you get started. Ideally, the book will become a taxonomy that you can easily tailor using your own creativity and knowledge.

In summary, there is something for leaders in each phase of their personal journey. Most leaders are lifelong learners. In fact, I've never met an effective leader who wasn't passionate about self-development and mastering the art of leading people to accomplish great things.

President Kennedy recognized this. In remarks focused on national security, intended to be delivered on that fateful 1963 day in Dallas, he would have said in that distinctive Boston accent that if Americans are not guided by the "lights of learning and reason, they would risk falling for the simple solutions and rhetoric of demagogues."

In fact, it is the most quoted line from this famous, but never delivered, speech that gives me reason to write this book: "Leadership and learning are indispensable to each other." [3]

How to Get the Most From the Book

The leadership journey demands continuous learning. For many, it begins when we are young and continues throughout our professional lives. Others find themselves at a career or life midpoint when they are unexpectedly invited to manage people, guide a project, or

---

3   John F. Kennedy, "Remarks prepared for delivery at the Trade Mart in Dallas, TX," November 22, 1963, available at https://www.jfklibrary.org/archives/other-resources/john-f-kennedy-speeches/dallas-tx-trade-mart-undelivered-19631122 (Accessed January 2021).

harness the energies of fellow volunteers in a ministry or community-based effort. In any case, the journey begins somewhere.

The leadership journey rarely has a clear destination. It tends to continue, taking us to different places along the way as promotions come, jobs change, and opportunities emerge. Some prepare diligently for the different legs of their journey, while others are thrust into a leadership role and learn by doing. I'm a proponent of structured training, but I have found that the daily activities and interactions of leadership, when mindfully engaged, can more powerfully propel us forward than waiting for a class, coach, or instructor to give direction.

Every leadership path involves people and a need to get things done. Both components carry equal weight and deserve equal consideration. The following chapters offer insights and an invitation to reflect on different aspects of people and performance. Some chapters focus more on one than the other, but there is always a link between the two primary drivers of leadership success.

As you read, you may sense tension between the two. If so, I invite you to embrace the tension and think deeply about what some might label paradoxical – the ability to consistently meet the needs of people while fearlessly pursuing big goals. You might also encounter the false dilemma of thinking it's got to be one or the other. At a minimum, you'll be tempted to say at some point, "but something's got to give." Instead, I encourage you to wrestle with the most important question: How do I do both?

Because thinking deeply and wrestling with challenging ideas is hard work, I recommend you read a chapter a day, or even one a week, instead of trying to race through the book. There are no prizes for speed reading. In each chapter, I'll ask you to engage with the material in some way – usually through some reflection questions and action items. None will be too demanding or time consuming, but all are designed to help you connect a concept to something relevant. Making this connection to your world is how learning happens for adults.

Ultimately, this book is intended to help you become a better leader, so put the ideas to work and make them useful early and often. Don't hesitate to try a recommendation, perhaps even in a challenging situation. Be open to adjusting the way you lead – the way you interact with people. Who knows? You might see results right away.

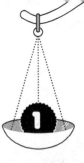

getting started

WHAT'S IT LIKE to be on the other end of you? Let's begin with a simple experiment. Recall the worst leader you have **personally** encountered in your professional life. Exclude current or recently departed politicians, grand-scale megalomaniacs, and anyone responsible for mass murder unless, of course, you had a personal connection to them. I'm talking about that really bad boss with whom you crossed paths regularly.

Despite taking those go-to options off the table, you're still likely to come up with several good candidates rather quickly. From the clueless kid in his first management role to the control freak who micromanaged your every move, weigh your options carefully. Certainly, don't overlook the political animal who injured her shoulder throwing people under the bus because she, too, might be a good choice for what's coming. If you've been around a while, it may be difficult to choose just one of these lousy characters, but please try.

Do you see that person's face in your mind's eye? If so, you are likely starting to recall some of your interactions with them. What are you feeling? Even though you may be muttering obscenities or breaking out in a cold sweat right about now as you recall your time in that person's orbit, please embrace what you're feeling.

exercise

In the margin of the page or on a separate sheet of paper, write five words that describe how you felt when you were around this person.

When I've done this as a flip chart or whiteboard activity with groups, I saw these words:

- Small
- Weak
- Anxious
- Cautious
- Frustrated
- Voiceless
- Powerless
- Stuck
- Disengaged
- Sick
- Exhausted
- Drained
- Disgusted
- Confused
- Embarrassed
- Fearful
- Angry
- Insufficient

Do any of them fit you? Feel free to use them if they reflect how you felt around that leader, or come up with your own. Be sure to write them down.

Now, think about the best leader you've personally known. How did you feel around them? Here are some words that might fit (circle any that apply), or again, add to the list:

- Inspired
- Empowered
- Engaged
- Included
- Confident
- Conscientious
- Accountable
- Enthusiastic
- Optimistic
- Focused
- Committed
- Positive
- Loyal
- Trusting
- Devoted
- Energized
- Cared for
- Informed

A huge difference, right? But what makes that difference? That's what we'll explore in the pages that follow.

Feelings are one thing, but you also had to get something done while associated with these people, right? Few organizations invite you to join their payroll for the purpose of building your social network. You had to fill your role in the mission.

Now, return to the worst and best leaders you identified a moment ago. How did each team perform? Use whatever metrics make the most sense: revenue, productivity, on-time completion of projects, etc. You might also consider which leader's team had higher turnover. Which team spawned more complaints for HR to sort through? Now, give those leaders letter grades for their ability to get things done and everything else you considered. Use the old A-to-F system that most of us are familiar with from our school days.

I've done this group exercise hundreds of times over the years. Predictably, I hear a lot of C, D, and F grades on the performance of the bad leaders, but much better grades for the good ones.

This supports my assertion that teams perform better when leaders create a positive environment for their people.

If my anecdotal evidence isn't enough, let's consider the findings of a few of the most respected thinkers in the field, like Amy Cuddy of Harvard Business School. Professor Cuddy and her research colleagues found that leaders who projected warmth—even before their technical competence, skill, and mental toughness were revealed—were perceived as influential and trustworthy, two factors directly linked to superior performance. On the other hand, leaders who were perceived as competent, but lacking in humanity, often were resented.[1]

Occasionally, I will hear from some outliers who claim their manager, Attila the Hun, actually got good results while treating the team like unwashed peasants and undermining colleagues right and left. This is rarely the case, though. Researchers Jack Zenger and Joseph Folkman studied the effectiveness of 51,836 leaders. They discovered that only 27 who ranked in the bottom quartile on the likability scale were also in the top 25 percent in overall. If you do the math, you'll find that you have a 1 in 2,000 chance of being both nasty and a great leader.[2]

In my experience, it's far more likely to hear people speak in almost reverent tones – often with a great deal of emotion – about the times in their careers when they were part of a truly great team that achieved extraordinary results. Its manager was approachable, treated everyone with dignity and respect, and somehow knew how to bring out the best in each person. In the stories I've heard, there is often a line about how much fun it was to work with **those** people and accomplish **so** much.

Sadly, many people long for such leadership again in their present work setting, while others who have never experienced such positivity may wonder if it's even possible.

---

1 Amy J.C. Cuddy, Matthew Kohut, & John Neffinger, "Connect, then lead," *Harvard Business Review*, July-August 2013, available at https://hbr.org/2013/07/connect-then-lead (Accessed January 27, 2021).

2 Jack Zenger and Joseph Folkman, "I'm The Boss! Why Should I Care If You Like Me?" *Harvard Business Review*, May 2, 2013, available at https://hbr.org/2013/05/im-the-boss-why-should-i-care (Accessed January 27, 2021).

Rather than wallow in nostalgia, why not be an agent of change? Recognize that **you** can create that positive environment for the people you lead.

The first step is to ask yourself, "What's it like to be on the other end of me?"

If the answer is anything less than incredible, you have some work to do. The good news is that you are creating those impressions and crafting your culture in each interaction you have today. The balancing act of people and performance is happening now, so there is no time to waste.

reflection

Take all the time needed to answer the following questions about the impression you make on your team and other co-workers. Try to think of specific examples that support your answers because they will serve as evidence that you are on the right path or show the need for adjustments.

- Think about the key people on your team. What feelings would they express after interacting with you? Are you comfortable with the descriptive words they used?
- How do you want to be described as a leader?

- Are you creating an environment where your team can thrive? What evidence do you have to support your answer?
- What have you learned from some of the best and worst leaders you have served under?
- What mechanisms are in place for you to receive honest feedback? How are you taking advantage of them?

Your honest answers to these questions say a lot about whether you are creating an environment in which your people can perform at their best. If you think you can do better in any area, develop a specific action plan. The list of **action items** below will help you get started.

action items

Reflect on the questions above, then choose one or more of the action items below as your to-do list this week or this month. Work through the list to refine best practices that work for you. Consistency and making habits of these actions will produce better results.

- Ask for feedback. It can come through a structured process like a 360-degree assessment – if that's available to you – or you can simply ask the people around you to give it to you straight. You might start with your manager and peers, but direct reports can be the most important source of feedback on your leadership. There are no magic words. It can be as simple as, "Be honest. How do you think am I doing?"

  Of course, you will want to make it safe for them to

speak freely by promising no hurt feelings or repercussions. Explain that you respect their judgment and that their honest feedback would be a very generous gift. If you sense hesitation or discomfort, that may be a more powerful message than any words.

• In a future team meeting, let people know that you're working on your leadership skills and would appreciate their help. Invite their honest observations and let them know that you are a work in progress. Actually, we all are. Depending on your past behavior, some people might be skeptical, but be sincere, be transparent, and be encouraged, because you're doing the right thing.

• Help the author expand his research by emailing the five words you used to describe how you felt after interacting with the best and worst leaders you considered in this chapter. Send those descriptive words to mike@drmikepatterson.com.

additional reading

Thanks for the Feedback: The Science and Art of Receiving Feedback Well, Douglas Stone and Sheila Heen, Penguin Books; 1st edition (March 4, 2014)

"I'm the Boss! Why Should I Care If You Like Me?", Jack Zenger and Joseph Folkman, *Harvard Business Review*, May 2, 2013

what's the mission?

the north star that provides direction

I T WAS A hot, steamy July day when my mother invited me and my friend, Bobby, into our air-conditioned family room to watch what she called "history in the making." Mom rarely made such big pronouncements, so I suspected that whatever we were about to see would be really big. Besides, I generally was expected to be outdoors on sunny days, roaming the neighborhood from about 9 a.m. until dark—with allowances for lunch and dinner, of course.

Bobby and I sat on the floor about 2 feet from the giant console television that consumed a good portion of the room, initially watching a static CBS News simulation of the lunar module sitting on the surface of the moon. Even by the standards of the day, it wasn't terribly exciting. And then, cutting through the commentators' chatter, we heard astronaut Neil Armstrong say, "Houston, Tranquility Base here. The Eagle has landed."[1]

For reasons I didn't fully understand at the time, I knew these words were momentous. That was confirmed when the cameras cut back to the two newsmen on the set, who were momentarily speech-

1   NASA, Apollo 11 Mission Overview, available at https://www.nasa.gov/mission_pages/apollo/missions/apollo11.html (Accessed 16 January 2021).

less and wiping their eyes. Soon, we started to see live, greenish-gray images of the moon's surface, and it was exciting to get a ringside view of the moon we saw each night from 240,000 miles away.

Several hours later, I squinted at grainy black-and-white images to see Armstrong and fellow astronaut Buzz Aldrin leave the lunar module to walk on the moon. With his first step, Armstrong famously said, "That's one small step for man, one giant leap for mankind."[2]

Our missions at work may not have the historical significance of a moon landing; nonetheless, they are important within the workplace. The problem is that the vision of what we need to accomplish is often less clear than the goal President Kennedy outlined in a 1961 joint session of Congress. With such clarity, he made it obvious what should consume the people at NASA for the rest of the decade, let Congress know that they would need to loosen their purse strings to fund the grand project, and broadcast to the world—especially Soviet Union leader Nikita Khrushchev—that America was going to be the dominant superpower. The mission sends a message.

In the pages that follow, I will make the case for describing your mission so clearly that everyone involved understands what needs to get done and adjusts their behavior to make it happen. In that regard, simple is best. I have sat through far too many meetings with high-priced consultants, haggling for days with my peers over the wording of mission, vision, and value statements. Oftentimes, those off-site parsing parties produce minimal results. We might print posters to

---

2 NASA, July 20, 1969: One Giant Leap for Mankind, available at https://www.nasa.gov/mission_pages/apollo/apollo11.html (Accessed 16 January 2021).

place in headquarters' common areas and occasionally add fancy words to the company website, but that's about it. All we had to show for the tedious hours of wordsmithing were the words themselves, a big invoice from the consultant (sorry, consultants), and a few extra pounds from the food and drink we consumed at the resort where we met. We often fail to recognize that the only metric that matters is whether the mission is accomplished, and that only happens if everyone knows their role and responds accordingly.

In the present context, a **mission** is a clear, concise statement that describes what must be done—the North Star that guides your actions as a leader and directs the daily activities of your team. It represents what is important when it comes to results.

The word "mission" may be used to describe a brief burst of effort to achieve a particular outcome. For example, the U.S. Secret Service's mission in the month of January every four years is to secure the inauguration to allow for a peaceful transfer of power from president to president. A mission can also be longstanding and ongoing, as in: Since 1902, a primary mission of the Secret Service has been to protect U.S. presidents. Only two agents were assigned to the White House detail during Theodore Roosevelt's presidency versus the hundreds of agents who protect the president today,[3] showing that missions can expand, change, or be completed, making them no longer necessary. Nevertheless, your entire team needs to know the mission and how they contribute to its completion.

---

3 United States Secret Service, History, available at https://www.secretservice.gov/about/history (Accessed 19 January 2021).

I concede that my definition of **mission** is similar to how many define **goal**. A goal, according to Merriam-Webster, is "the end toward which effort is directed."[4] The words can even interchange in some situations. I like mission, though, because it suggests gravity and certainty, whereas a goal is something we may or may not achieve.

As you read the following paragraphs about the power and purpose of having a well-defined mission, think about how you have been communicating with your people about what's most important. Does everyone know what they are working toward or do some show up and wait for the phone to ring or something to land in their email inbox to guide their day? Would your people better manage their tasks and time if they more clearly understood the mission? Is your team laser focused on what matters most? Additional reflection questions and action items can be found at the end of this chapter.

Remember, don't hurry through this book. Read reflectively and work to connect the ideas I'll present with your current practices. If you read only one chapter this week, that's okay, especially if you were able to try something you read with your team. In other words, these suggestions only have value if you can apply them to **your** mission.

A mission keeps people focused. While scrolling through the cable channels a few weeks ago, I stumbled across one of my all-time favorite movies, *The Blues Brothers*. I've seen the 1980 classic at least a dozen times, but it always makes me laugh—and think.

---

4 Merriam-Webster Dictionary, available at https://www.merriam-webster.com/dictionary/goal (Accessed 18 January 2021).

If you haven't seen the movie, the basic storyline is this: Jake and Elwood Blues, played by John Belushi and Dan Aykroyd, respectively, are ne'er-do-well R&B musicians who return to the Catholic orphanage where they grew up to learn it will soon be shuttered if an overdue county tax bill isn't paid in short order. That means the current crop of orphans will be put out on the streets, and the Blues brothers' boyhood home will be no more. After an emotional experience in a lively church service led by a pastor played by none other than James Brown, the brothers find themselves on a "mission from God." That mission drives and sustains them through a series of misadventures as they revive the band to save the orphanage. I won't spoil the movie for you, but suffice it to say, their mission keeps the brothers focused.

In matters both big and small, focus is essential. Imagine arriving on the first tee of a beautiful, immaculately maintained golf course with a brand-new set of the latest clubs and a dozen tournament-quality golf balls ready to be lofted onto pristine fairways. You're excited to finally put all of the lessons with your top-notch instructor to use, but as you lean down to tee up your first shot, you realize that you have no idea of the green's location. There are no flags in sight and no out-of-bounds stakes. The other people in your foursome don't seem to know either. So, where do you aim?

This can, unfortunately, be the case for new employees who show up ready to play the game of their lives. If they don't clearly understand the mission and strategy, they will hit more than a few errant shots. Moreover, they may even leave prematurely with a vow to tell everyone they know that your course—or company—is horrible. Who needs that?

Without mission awareness, it's also easy to become distracted. Big distractions often show up as a great new opportunity that **everyone** seems to be jumping on. It could very well be the next big thing, but this exciting new path could end abruptly with you falling victim to shiny object syndrome, or SOS. Entrepreneurs and small-business owners seem most susceptible, perhaps because they aren't bound by corporate structure. After all, an entrepreneur is all about seizing the moment and flinging open doors of opportunity, right? A Fortune 500 battleship doesn't turn on a dime, meaning its middle managers can't easily pull the trigger on SOS ideas. There are, however, some infamous examples of CEOs doing so. Remember when Amazon and Facebook launched phones? Probably not. They both failed miserably.

A new pursuit can put you in real trouble if it isn't aligned with your overall mission or what you have identified to be your most important mission for this quarter or this year. Before you know it, you will have taken on too many new projects and will likely find yourself frustrated by the growing number of unfinished tasks and generally feeling overwhelmed. Maintaining focus on your present mission and saying "no" more often can help greatly. If it's not necessary to accomplish your current mission, do you need it?

Small distractions can also do big damage and often lurk at your fingertips. According to Udemy's 2018 Workplace Distraction Report,[5] 36 percent of millennials/Gen Zs spend two hours per workday looking at matters unrelated to work on their phones. Respondents from across the generations (86 percent) suggest that Facebook gets in the way of their work.

Distractions, whether driven by social media or a chatty coworker, can consume a lot of valuable time and, sadly, it can take people up to 30 minutes to get back on task. What a waste of time! Further bad news was reported by a team led by Gloria Mark from the University of California, Irvine.[6] She and her fellow researchers found that the need to compensate for distractions leads to higher levels of stress, frustration, and the perception that one's workload is overwhelming.

The point here is that getting people focused on their work requires a clear understanding of the mission—whether it's the grand mission of your organization or a micro-mission that needs to be accomplished today—your people deserve to understand what's important. The mission provides the best picture of what's important and helps us better manage our resources.

Mission determines resource allocation.

How you spend your time and money reflects who you are.

---

5 Udemy Research, 2018 Workplace Distraction Report, available at https://research. udemy.com/research_report/udemy-depth-2018-workplace-distraction-report/ (Accessed 18 January2021).

6 Mark, Gloria, et al. "Proceedings of the Sigchi Conference on Human Factors in Computing Systems." The Cost of Interrupted Work: More Speed and Stress, 2008, pp. 107–110.

Because both of these core resources—along with many others both tangible and intangible—are always limited, leaders spend much energy trying to figure out how best to use them. Without a clear mission to guide those investment decisions, vanity projects and personal preference can work their way into the resource allocation process. Worse, leaders may make spontaneous decisions based on how they're feeling in the moment. Neither serves the broader stakeholder community well nor leads to a good outcome.

More sophisticated investment models based on peak-year sales projections and five-year net present value, along with other factors like the technical complexity of projects, probabilities of success, and the competitive landscape are often useful in large enterprises with multimillion-dollar possibilities to weigh. Yet, even these resource allocation decisions often come down to charisma and forcefulness of the project advocates. Strong-willed leaders determined to get their way can hijack the process, no matter how strong the case for a different path. In the end, budget decisions become politicized and no one is happy.

Broad statements that describe a mission in sweeping terms like "increase shareholder value" or "improve patient lives" are of limited use and are nearly always coupled with more business jargon that does little to help people in the trenches make day-to-day decisions. On the other hand, a more clearly defined mission with specifically targeted outcomes allows for a results-focused approach. The mission, or what has to happen, drives the distribution of resources.

When the coronavirus pandemic forced schools across the nation to move learning online, students suddenly were required to have computers and access to the internet. This presented a major challenge for school districts serving less-affluent communities. Students without computers could not participate in classes and the school could not accomplish its mission. In Philadelphia, for example, the district purchased 50,000 Chromebooks for $11 million as part of its mandated shift to at-home learning.[7] Of course, the district couldn't have anticipated this need during 2019 budget sessions, but the mission made the decision clear.

On a smaller scale, the mission should influence how team members spend their time and organize their work. West Compass Insurance, a small firm in Southern California, adopted a mission to help its elderly clients choose the healthcare plan that best serves their unique needs and then maximize the value by accessing all available benefits. Its impact was immediate on how the firm's employees prioritized tasks and utilized their time.

Customer service agents were directed to go to any length to provide extraordinary service, no matter how much time was required. This meant waiting on hold for extended periods with carriers to answer a client's question about whether an obscure drug their doctor had prescribed was covered. Regularly, West Compass employees join their clients on calls with insurance companies to

7 Benjamin Herold, "Schools handed out millions of digital devices under COVID-19. Now, thousands are missing," *Education Week*, 23 July 2020, available at https://www. edweek.org/technology/schools-handed-out-millions-of-digital-devices-under-covid-19-now-thousands-are-missing/2020/07 (Accessed 20 January 2021)

navigate payment disputes. In one case, a conscientious customer service manager helped an elderly man with a toothache find a plan dentist who worked on Saturdays. This level of service comes at a cost to a company, but the mission makes the decision clear.

Missions make us happy. The pleasure of accomplishment is learned at a young age. If you're a parent, can you ever forget the unmitigated joy on your toddler's face when he or she took those first wobbly steps? Even though your little prince or princess may have traveled only a few feet before crashing, everyone present likely cheered as if the child had just won the Nobel Peace Prize. This affirmation leads to other attempts, more progress, and growth.

Throughout our lives, proud moments of achievement fuel us. Even when there is no one to cheer us on, the internal sense of accomplishment generates feelings of well-being and a drive to keep going. For most adults, work often provides the greatest opportunity to experience these feelings. Thus, knowing what is expected and whether you are meeting those standards are key sources of job satisfaction, according to the Happiness Research Institute,[8] an independent think tank in Denmark that researches well-being, happiness, and quality of life.

More precisely, a sense of accomplishment contributes to eudaemonic happiness, a concept that originated with philosophers like Aristotle, Plato, and Marcus Aurelius. This domain of happiness is related to meaning and purpose, while hedonic happiness is associ-

---

8   Happiness Research Institute, Job Satisfaction Index 2019, available at https://www.happinessresearchinstitute.com/publications/4579836749 (Accessed 21 January 2021)

ated with pleasure and enjoyment. Both are necessary to flourish in life, but philosophers argue that the eudaemonic domain is more virtuous. And who doesn't want to be more virtuous?

An understanding of personality theory—how people are wired—provides further insight into what motivates and energizes people. Some find enormous satisfaction in pressing toward a goal. When the goal is clear, each day's efforts can be measured, and they feel a sense of satisfaction or frustration, depending on the results. Others find fulfillment at work in other ways—crafting or improving a quality product, recognizing that their efforts have had a positive impact on people, or being part of a team that is operating with synergy. All, however, want to add value and contribute to a mission bigger than themselves.

Of course, you can't focus too much on feelings, but there are some major tangible benefits of being happy at work. At least that's what several economics professors from the University of Warwick in England found. Nose-to-the-grindstone types will be pleased to know that happy employees work harder and were about 12 percent more productive.[9] Other critical components of organizational success—like engagement, recruiting, and retention—all tend to improve when people perceive opportunities to accomplish a meaningful mission.

Many factors affect employee engagement. Some, like respect and trust, are very relational and are probably better addressed in

9 Oswald, Andrew J, et al. "Happiness and Productivity." Journal of Labor Economics, vol. 33, no. 4, 2015, pp. 789–822.

one of the "people always" chapters to come; others, including performance management, are truly relevant. Is the mission clear? Do I know my role? Am I aligned with my coworkers in our best attempt to accomplish the mission? Failure to put mission first will result in employee engagement issues.

An inspiring mission, lived out through the daily activities of the team, helps attract the right kind of talent.

Research from Deloitte, Robert Half, and others provides supporting data, but it's really just common sense to recognize that people are more inclined to join a firm involved in work they believe in versus joining an endeavor that is antithetical to who they are and what they believe.

This is especially true for millennials, who currently comprise the largest generational sector in the workforce, with about 75 million members in the U.S. alone. The Millennial Impact Report released by Achieve Consulting stated that 94 percent liked using their skills to support a cause.[10] Further research suggests it's not just millennials who want to be part of something meaningful. Sjoerd Gehring, vice president of talent acquisition and people experience at Johnson & Johnson, said "70 percent of U.S. adults say it is important to them

---

10 Kathy Gurckiek, "Millennials Desire to Do Good Defines Workplace Culture: Examine community service programs to 'seal the deal,'" Society for Human Resource Management, July 7, 2014, available at https://www.shrm.org/resourcesandtools/hr-topics/behavioral-competencies/global-and-cultural-effectiveness/pages/millennial-impact.aspx (Accessed 21 January 2021).

that their actions help make a positive difference in the world."[11] For me, this raises concern about the other 30 percent, but they probably wouldn't be a good fit anyway.

The evidence is clear. A sense of accomplishment produces happiness; however, there is no accomplishment where there is no mission. Acute mission focus attracts people who want to go all in for a cause, and it gives them reason to stay as long as they feel they are making a difference. A leader's commitment to the mission also influences the degree of trust among team members.

Fidelity to the mission engenders trust. Fidelity isn't a word we use much these days, but we should—because it means following through on commitments and remaining loyal. Pretty simple. Yet, how often are we left disappointed because people don't follow through or their actions don't line up with their words? Even omitting politicians from the conversation still leaves far too many people who fail to practice fidelity. It's tough to trust them and the organizations they represent.

The opposite is true when there is devotion to the mission.

Even as a former U.S. Army officer, I have tremendous respect for the Marines and their motto, *semper fidelis,* which is Latin for "always faithful." Since 1833, Marines have proudly proclaimed this promise to exemplify their commitment to win America's battles, as well as their pledge to look out for other Marines past and present.

---

11 Daniel Goleman, "Millennials: the purpose generation," KornFerry, available at https://www.kornferry.com/insights/articles/millennials-purpose-generation (Accessed 21 January 2021).

Far more than a marketing slogan, *semper fi* is a sacred vow that all Marines make.

The Marine Corps' values of honor, courage, and commitment were on full display during the Battle of Hue City in February 1968. Already wounded, Gunnery Sgt. John Canley repeatedly exposed himself to enemy fire and continued the fight in order to pull other wounded Marines to safety. Former President Trump ultimately presented Canley with the Congressional Medal of Honor, and the accompanying citation concluded with: "Then-Gunnery Sgt. Canley's heroic actions saved the lives of his teammates."[12]

Semper fi.

Of course, that isn't to suggest that all leaders should risk life and limb to prove their commitment to the cause; however, I do believe leaders should demonstrate fidelity by doing all they can to accomplish the mission and take care of their people. If they don't do those two basic things, they risk losing the trust of their followers.

Mission helps you keep score, but it isn't always about money. We have already established that a sense of accomplishment is a critical component of well-being and professional pride. These are intrinsic factors for many people, but some simply enjoy keeping score. It's difficult to imagine elite athletes engaged in a game without the score being kept. The best enjoy testing their skills—sometimes against

---

12 Marines: The Official Website of the United States Marine Corps, "Medal of Honor: Sgt. Maj. John Canley," available at https://www.marines.mil/News/Press-Releases/Press-Release-Display/Article/1644927/medal-of-honor-sgt-maj-john-canley/#:~:text=-Canley%2C%20United%20States%20Marine%20Corps,in%20the%20Republic%20of%20Vietnam (Accessed 21 January 2021).

others in competition, but often **with** others to solve a problem or overcome a challenge. A well-defined mission provides opportunities to measure success, evaluate effort, and determine whether you and your team are improving along the way.

A highlight of my professional life was the day I spent with legendary basketball coach John Wooden. Of course, many sports fans know Wooden as the Wizard of Westwood, who won ten NCAA championships over a 12-year period as head coach of the UCLA Bruins. His former players like Bill Walton and Kareem Abdul-Jabbar know him as the man who changed their lives. At one point during his long tenure, Wooden won 88 consecutive games, and he had four perfect 30-0 seasons. "Coach" was well into his 90s and becoming frail by the time I met him, but the strength of his character filled the room.

During our session, Coach Wooden spoke little about championships or records; instead, he spoke at length about his life as a teacher who emphasized hard work and the importance of **always** giving one's best effort. This mission governed his behavior and was the foundation for his famous definition of success: "Success is the peace of mind, which is the direct result of self-satisfaction in knowing you made the effort to do your best to become the best that you are capable of becoming."[13] Wooden's mission was to help young men become successful in life; winning basketball games was simply a means to that end.

---

13 John Wooden & Jay Carty, *Coach Wooden's Pyramid of Success: Building Blocks for a Better Life.* California: Gospel Light Publications, 2005, p. 12.

Coach Wooden is also a good example of how money can't buy the peace of mind represented in his definition of success, nor can it serve as the best source of motivation for people. According to the *Los Angeles Times*, John Wooden was paid $6,000 in 1948, his first year of coaching the Bruins. Adjusted for inflation, that's about $58,000. In 1975, the year that Coach Wooden won his tenth NCAA championship, he made a whopping $40,500, or about $175,000 in inflation-adjusted dollars.[14] It's also rumored that, along the way, he turned down an offer to coach the Los Angeles Lakers at a salary ten times his pay at UCLA. While it's a far cry from the mindset of most players, coaches, and business executives today, money simply didn't motivate Coach Wooden.

Don't get me wrong. In capitalistic, free-market societies, people should make as much as they can and not turn down opportunities to make substantially more. However, those who lead service or knowledge-based employees—now about 70 percent of the workforce, according to Deloitte[15]—should recognize that higher pay is not a certain path to improved performance or sustained engagement. Compensation is a complicated topic that must include consideration of an employee's motives, goals, and expectations. Certain teachers and religious workers give themselves wholeheartedly to their respective causes despite comparatively low pay.

---

14 Bill Dwyer, "Steve Alford's salary is 14.8 times higher than John Wooden's pay," *Los Angeles Times*, July 12, 2013 (Accessed January 22, 2021).

15 Lisa Barry, "Performance management is broken," Deloitte Insights (Accessed 23 January 2021).

The fallacy that more money leads to better performance relies on behavioral psychology, a theory largely developed from the study of laboratory animals. Although I've never managed lab animals, my experience with people suggests that a simple stimulus-response model falls woefully short when trying to explain humans' complex system of motives and needs.

Study after study bears this out, dating back to a massive 1985 meta-analysis conducted by Richard Guzzo of the University of Maryland, College Park, and colleagues from New York University.[16] After examining 98 different studies, researchers found no significant effect for the financial incentives presented. They also found that none of the interventions materially improved absenteeism and turnover. Instead, they found far more evidence to support investments in talent development, goal setting, and coaching.

Of course, there is a place and purpose for compensation management (Yes, incentive and comp managers, we need you!). To attract and retain talent requires paying people fairly. Nevertheless, the simple point here is that compensation management cannot work unless there is first clarity around the mission.

In short, money without mission makes no sense.

Mission first is a testimony to the fact that without a clear understanding of what you're there to do, your role as a leader is reduced to

---

16 Guzzo, Richard A, et al. "The Effects of Psychologically Based Intervention Programs on Worker Productivity: A Meta-Analysis." *Personnel Psychology*, vol. 38, no. 2, 1985, pp. 275–291., doi:10.1111/j.1744-6570.1985.tb00547.x.

that of social director. People must recognize what needs to be done before the right things can happen. This demands that the leader's first job is to make sure the mission is clear and understood by all. It is only with that clarity of focus that great things can be accomplished.

That first moon landing and safe return of the astronauts was more than 50 years ago and was the culmination of President Kennedy's clarion call to action years before. Now, with its Artemis II mission, NASA will be joined by commercial and international partners in sending four astronauts back to the moon. The 10-day mission is planned for 2024 and will be an important step toward human travel to Mars.[17] Undoubtedly, much has changed since Neil Armstrong made that first small step in 1969. But as my grandchildren tune in on various digital devices to watch the next group of intrepid space travelers step onto the moon, one thing remains the same: The mission is first.

reflection

Spend as much time as needed to answer the following questions about your mission and how well you communicate it to your team. Try to think of specific examples that support your answers because

---

17 National Aeronautics and Space Administration, Artemis Plan: NASA's Lunar Exploration Program Overview, September 2020, available at https://www.nasa.gov/artemisprogram (Accessed 19 January 2021).

they will serve as evidence that you are on the right path or make the case for some necessary adjustments.

- How have you seen your mission in action lately?
- When is the last time you talked about mission topics with your team? On any given day, could team members tell you how their work contributes to the current mission?
- How do mission needs influence how you manage time and allocate your budget?
- How much time are team members spending on tasks that aren't critical to the mission? What distractions keep them from focusing on the mission? Have you discussed this with them lately? Do you need to redirect their efforts in any way?
- What should you do to ensure the people on your team understand the mission and their role in accomplishing it? Is this part of your onboarding process?
- When did you last have a mission-accomplished celebration to recognize a win—big or small?

Your honest answers to these questions say a lot about whether you have created a mission-first culture. If you think you can do better, develop a specific action plan to drive your growth in the area you see as lacking. The action items below will help you get started.

action items

Choose one or more of the action items below to tackle this week or this month. Work through the list to refine best practices that work for you. If you are consistent and make habits of these actions, you will see better results.

- Without being confrontational, poll your team to determine what they believe is their mission on any given day or week. If there is hesitance, uncertainty, or wide variation across the group, help them become clear on the mission and the behaviors necessary to achieve it.
- Do mission check-ins during weekly staff meetings or daily standups. Ensure that your people are prioritizing mission-first behaviors and seek to understand any hindrances.
- Begin each coaching session with team members by focusing on the mission. Ask some form of the question, "What are you trying to accomplish?"
- Sales team members likely have some combination of revenue, market share, or customer retention goals on which they are evaluated and compensated. Develop, share, and monitor the mission-essential behaviors that lead to sales success. Depending on your particular situation, this list should include activity metrics like calls per day, emails per

day, sales presentations per week, the use of certain sales collateral, etc. The key is that they clearly understand the mission-essential behaviors that lead to sales effectiveness.

- Keep a log of how you use your time in a given day, week, or month. If you are spending a lot of time on things that aren't essential to the mission, adjust to invest your most precious resource on mission-related priorities. If administrative mandates or unrelated tasks are consuming a lot of your time, discuss this with your manager or senior leadership. You can't accomplish the mission without being mindful of your time.

- When your team achieves a significant mission-related milestone, celebrate it together—and find creative ways to include team members who work remotely.

additional reading

The 7 Habits of Highly Effective People, Stephen R. Covey, 4th Edition, Simon and Schuster, 2020

Start with Why: How Great Leaders Inspire Everyone to Take Action, Simon Sinek, Portfolio, 2011

Free to Focus: A Total Productivity System to Achieve More by Doing Less, Michael Hyatt, Baker Books, 2019

"Don't Let Opportunism Compromise Your Corporate Mission," *Harvard Business Review*, Graham Kenny, June 3, 2020.

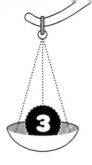

why does the mission matter?
how to create a culture of commitment

T O LEARN ABOUT commitment, it's helpful to focus on beer. Granted, learning and libation typically don't travel hand in hand. However, I can think of no one better to teach important lessons about commitment than a brewmaster whose name is known worldwide—Mr. Arthur Guinness.

Guinness, a national hero in his homeland of Ireland, founded his famous brewery in 1752 near Leixlip. Like many entrepreneurs today, he started with a big dream but a small bank account. Fortunately, Guinness inherited some money from a local archbishop of the Church of Ireland that he used as seed money. At age 34, Guinness was so confident of succeeding that he famously signed a 9,000-year lease for a yearly sum of 45 British pounds, or about 60 U.S. dollars at today's exchange rate. This was on St. James Gate, where the brewery still stands.

Within a few years, Guinness had taken the dilapidated equipment he found in the old buildings, added to it, developed his skills, and begun exporting beer to England. The market's thirst for a rich porter made from roasted barley created a sales spike for the dark, aromatic brew. Guinness enjoyed the success of his hard work before his death in 1803, but he couldn't have known his name would be recognized worldwide, nor that his business would continue to thrive more than 250 years after its founding.

What Arthur Guinness did know was that he was "called" to make a positive impact on the world. Beer and business success were simply a means to that end. This calling was the internal drive that kept Guinness going, even in the face of difficulty. This same principle—the importance of knowing one's why—is still at work today, although now we have science to help us understand how it works.

But first, a bit more about the man behind the brand.

Guinness was a devout Christian whose vibrant faith was fed by the powerful preaching of men like John and Charles Wesley, and George Whitefield. Their mantra during this season of Great Awakening was not only a call for commitment to Jesus Christ, but also to serve one's community. Whitefield led by example, founding several orphanages, supporting feeding centers for the poor, and even challenging sinful social institutions like slavery when he visited the American colonies.

Transformed by this mindset of service, Guinness recognized that his passion and skills as a beer maker could be honed to combat some of the major social problems of his city. One of the ways he did this was by positioning beer as a healthy alternative. That's hard to fathom from a 21st-century perspective, but it was absolutely true of the people of 18th-century Europe—especially the poor.

Sanitation was quite lacking in crowded, low-income neighborhoods, and the available drinking water directly caused many ailments. In response, people began concocting high-alcohol gin at home—often in their bathtubs. Of course, this bathtub gin came with its own set of concerns, such as public drunkenness and abuse in the home. Recognizing this problem, Guinness presented his product as a more nutritious, less expensive, and safer alternative to hard liquor, while its lower alcohol content made it a better option for those without clean drinking water.

The beer-for-health concept caught on and helped curb alcoholism and associated evils. Guinness's business success created opportunities for him to serve the most vulnerable citizens of his city in other ways, as well. In addition to opening Sunday Schools to spread the Gospel and provide rudimentary education to children, he sat on the board of Meath Hospital, which focused on providing free healthcare in the poorest parts of Dublin.

In the decades after Arthur's death, the company he had founded would be a standard bearer for progressive employment practices by providing affordable housing, pensions, and 24-hour health (and dental) care for employees and their families. To this day, Guinness remains a premier employer in Dublin, with employees known to be passionate about their work and zealously committed to their company. This loyalty also shows up in the community.

Simply having a rock-solid mission that is clearly communicated to everyone on the team does not guarantee widespread devotion.

> *Commitment and accountability only occur when people are able to connect their personal motivation—their why—to their work, as Arthur Guinness did.*

When the mission becomes personal, then it's hard to pull them off task. In short, people commit when the mission matters—to them.

Commitment also brings ownership and initiative. Small-business owners or entrepreneurs are often the first to arrive and last to leave, constantly working for the success—or survival—of their business. From cleaning restrooms to learning new software, they do whatever is needed. What leader wouldn't want a team filled with folks who own their work and willingly take initiative? The key to developing this level of commitment is to tap into the right kind of motivation.

Edward Deci and Richard Ryan are two scholars who study different forms of motivation. They are particularly well known for their research on self-determination theory (SDT), a broad framework for the study of human motivation and personality.[1] Their work explores different types of motivation and their power to drive behavior. One critical lesson that SDT teaches is why "carrots and sticks" often fail as managerial tools. We get there by understanding the differences between extrinsic and intrinsic motivation.

---

1 Center for Self-Determination Theory, The Theory, available at https://selfdetermina-tiontheory.org/the-theory/ (Accessed January 25, 2021).

Extrinsic motivation drives us to achieve external rewards. This is the thinking of executives whose intricate incentive plans reward people who meet certain performance objectives with salary increases, bonuses, trips, and assorted other alluring accolades. Now, some of you might be thinking, who wouldn't burn the midnight oil to earn an all-expenses-paid trip to Hawaii? For that matter, West Texas in August would be good as long as it comes with bragging rights. That's the carrot.

The stick taps into extrinsic motivation, as well, but it's the side that makes us want to avoid negative consequences. What parent hasn't, in a moment of exasperation, told a child, "If you don't..." followed by some horrible—at least from the child's perspective—form of punishment? Some examples: If you don't get in the car right now, we're not getting ice cream! If you don't clean your room, no video games for a week!

Of course, we threaten people with the stick at work, too.

To be honest, carrots and sticks do seem to affect behavior for a time, but their impact is temporary, and they almost always fail at the worst possible time. That's why we need to understand there's a more powerful form of motivation that comes from the inside. Intrinsic motivation comes from our core values, personality, and sense of morality. This is what inspired Guinness to use his beer business to improve the health and welfare of the poorest people in Dublin.

Scholars say internal drives are so powerful because, when we act on them, we feel more aligned with who we believe we really are (sometimes called "ideal self") rather than feeling controlled by someone else and conforming to their standards.

Deci and Ryan are even more precise when they identify three needs that, when met, drive commitment and engagement, eliminating the need for carrots and sticks.

- Autonomy: When people feel they control their own destiny and can make their own decisions.
- Competence: When people feel capable of performing tasks that are important to them.
- Relatedness: When people feel connected to and cared for by others.[2]

While the importance varies from one personality type to another, all three of these needs must be met to some extent for people to thrive and do their best work. The degree to which they are met also determines whether team members are willing to go all in for the mission. Likewise, a lack of commitment places the mission at risk.

This link between commitment and performance made me hungry to learn more about the factors that affect commitment in organizations. My study, conducted in May 2016 while I was a leader at Core Strengths, included 1,849 responses to an online survey of adults working in the corporate sector in the United States.[3] The findings provided five indicators that workplace commitment is at risk:

---

2 Edward Deci, Richard Ryan. *Handbook of Self-Determination Research*. Rochester, NY: *The University of Rochester Press*, 2002.

3 Michael Patterson, *How to Inspire Personal Responsibility in Your Organization*, 2016 Workplace Commitment Study. Carlsbad: Personal Strengths Publishing, 2016. Note: Many of the ideas and findings from this

1. People don't follow through. Survey respondents widely reported (98.2%) they felt personally responsible for results. People certainly need to feel some sense of responsibility for outcomes; however, in a business context, it seems more important that they actually deliver. Without delivery of a desired outcome, a commitment is simply an empty promise.

With this in mind, I wanted to understand who could be counted on to fulfill their promises by actually delivering results. Not surprisingly, those who responded to the survey believed they were most reliable, with 55.6% of the 1,849 respondents claiming that they always deliver on their commitments. Yet, the reliability of others was rated far lower, raising key questions about trust and organizational culture that we'll address later in the book.

Specifically, peers were rated lowest, with only 10% always delivering on commitments. Organizational leaders followed closely, with just 13.2% always coming through. These dismal numbers reflect broad skepticism and reinforce the old adage "talk is cheap."

When asked whether team performance would improve if everyone simply fulfilled their commitments, 76.4% of respondents believed it would, while 17.4% were uncertain. Only 6.2% of respondents believed that fulfilling commitments would have no impact on team performance. This suggests that two things are negatively impacting the mission everywhere: failure to follow through and a reluctance to count on team members.

---

research are presented here with the permission of Core Strengths.

Furthermore, these results indicate that a lack of personal, individual accountability can hurt an organization's chances for success. With peers and leaders viewed as least reliable, it is possible that expectations are misaligned, or people simply tend to overrate their own efforts in comparison to others. Either way, this perception cripples overall organizational performance and suggests a real need to develop personal accountability throughout the organization—to help team members clearly understand their own commitments and others' expectations.

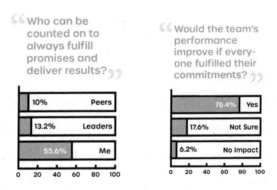

2. Work is not seen as personally important. In part, the survey was designed to explore whether people commit more fully when their daily work is meaningful. The responses (91.3%) made it clear that commitment levels are certainly greater when tasks carry a higher degree of personal importance. Furthermore, 98.3% of employees said they are willing to take on difficult or more challenging tasks—and see them through to completion—when they see the task as personally important. In other words, when people engage intrinsic motivation, commitment grows.

This suggests that tapping into intrinsic motivation—a person's core reasons—is a means for engaging commitment, persistence, and resilience.

It also illustrates the importance of helping people explore their motives and values, and then equipping them to determine what's important to them and their daily tasks.

For example, does a customer service representative see her work as an opportunity to help clients access products and services that improve their lives? If helping people is something she values, then every customer interaction is an opportunity to live out her personal values. According to the survey data, she is more likely to be committed to her work, and more willing to deal with difficult customers and go the extra mile to make sure they are ultimately satisfied.

Let's say a salesperson is motivated by competition and results, like gaining market share from a competitor or winning a company-sponsored sales contest. He fully commits to opportunities that satisfy his personal values. At the same time, he may not be energized by completing expense reports and capturing notes from sales calls. But if he can connect those tasks to what he ultimately values—performance—then he will bring the same level of commitment as he does to more competitive opportunities.

Key elements, then, for creating a culture of commitment, are letting people discover what drives them, having a common language to articulate these priorities, and encouraging team members to connect their daily tasks and personal values. Commitment will then naturally occur without a need for extreme controls or incentives, because the most powerful force—their motives—resides within each team member.

3. People lack interpersonal skills. The research also examined the relationship between workplace interactions and job performance—specifically:

- Whether people thought their interactions with colleagues impacted their effectiveness on the job.
- How respondents viewed their own relational skills.
- If they adjust their approach based on the task or the people involved.

Nearly all respondents (95.9%) agreed that the quality of their work relationships plays a major role in the overall quality of their work. If that is true, then it is absolutely critical to teach employees the skills to communicate, collaborate, and resolve problems with others. And yet, only 20.5% of respondents strongly agreed that they know how to bring out the best in others at work. Only 39.9% reported always modifying their approach based on the people involved. Some situations don't require behavioral adjustments, but most do. How often do we interact with people who think, communicate, and feel exactly like we do?

One explanation for the lack of relational agility is the aforementioned lack of confidence in knowing how to bring out the best in others. Another is that people simply don't know what matters to others.

I asked several questions to gauge if respondents were aware of their colleagues' priorities. Specifically, I wanted to know if they understood what was important to their managers and direct reports, and if they felt their manager knew what was important to them.

The results reveal a perceived gap—greatest at the managerial level—as 44.7% of respondents either do not believe or are unsure their manager knows their priorities. Likewise, only 22.2% of managers strongly agreed they knew what was most important to their team members.

This may explain why employees often leave organizations over conflict with their immediate supervisors. Furthermore, research[4] reveals a direct connection between employee engagement and turnover—and inadequate support from the immediate supervisor. If a manager does not provide clear expectations, support, and opportunities for development, the employee will have a poor view of their role and value to the organization, and quickly move on to where they can be more effective.

The results also captured an intriguing contradiction. While only 22.2% of managers strongly agreed they know what is important to their employees, a higher percentage of employees said they did feel understood by their managers. This, too, raises some interesting questions:

- Are managers "faking it" by giving the impression they understand their employees' priorities when they really don't?

---

4 R. Finnegan. *Rethinking retention: In good times and bad, breakthrough ideas for keeping your best workers.* Boston: Davies-Black, 2010.

· Are employees giving managers undue credit and assuming they are understood when they really aren't?

Both of these possibilities speak to the importance of clear and authentic communication, as well as the need for a common language when seeking to retain, engage, and inspire employees. Not knowing what's important to people is costly. Managers cannot retain, engage, or inspire employees they do not know and understand. In short, relationships matter. Interactions send ripples far beyond what people initially perceive. Knowing how to engage people and what is important to them is the key to stronger results. Much like when traveling to a foreign country, speaking the local language leads to far richer and more interesting experiences than cobbling together a few commonly understood words. This certainly holds true for speaking to what energizes and interests a manager or direct report. Developing an understanding of each other leads to better interactions and stronger results.

4. Conflict is unchecked. The negative impact of interpersonal conflict was clearly portrayed in the survey, with 59.7% of respondents affirming the statement, "Interpersonal conflict hinders the performance of my team." Nearly half of the respondents (48.9%) also noted that interpersonal conflict made them feel less committed, and 88.7% said workplace conflict often arises over failure to deliver on commitments, as we touched on earlier. These results suggest an interrelated cycle of negative performance.

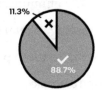

5. Accountability is enforced, not inspired. Only 19.2% of respondents strongly agreed that their manager carries primary responsibility for holding them accountable for their work, while 76.4% said individuals are mostly accountable to themselves.

These clear results fly in the face of most organizational efforts to train managers to hold employees accountable. Many of these programs are based on the premise that applying the right techniques and controls, and doling out the right mix of rewards and punishments, will keep employees in line. Most people, however, believe that accountability comes from within.

Since commitment is internally driven and created by and through a series of individual choices, it is foolish to think leaders can mandate buy-in. Still, there are actions leaders can take to create an environment where commitment is unwavering.

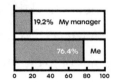

After this heavy-duty, data-driven discussion about commitment and how it affects performance, it's probably a good time to go back to the beer—figuratively speaking, of course. Earlier, we established that Arthur Guinness had incredible commitment inspired by his core values and lived out through his work in the community. This influenced the culture of his company and was not lost on future generations of leaders and employees.

With World War II raging—and particularly the Battle of Britain—tens of thousands left their homes to fight the Nazi on-slaught and protect the homeland. The British Expeditionary Force had been evacuated from Dunkirk, and France had fallen. Many feared that the German air force (Luftwaffe) would gain air superi-ority that would allow for a Nazi invasion. Every citizen across the British Isles was living in fear. The leaders of Guinness wanted to help the war effort, so they made a huge commitment, promising that every British soldier would enjoy a pint of Guinness—i.e., a taste of home—with his Christmas meal.

You might think, a beer company gave away some beer—big deal! But it was an extraordinary promise because Guinness had a big problem: Its workforce was depleted, as many employees were off at war. Working around the clock with a skeleton crew, they couldn't meet normal demand, much less produce enough extra beer for thousands upon thousands of soldiers to have a pint on Christmas.

What happened? With their clearly defined mission—every soldier gets a pint—they tapped into the power of commitment. The intrinsic motivation of their undersized staff fueled a volunteer effort that included Guinness retirees, workers from competing breweries, and even community members who wanted to have a hand in this noble cause. By working together, this diverse group of people accomplished the mission.

reflection

Spend as much time as needed to answer the following questions about how you are or are not tapping into intrinsic motivation to create a culture of commitment. Try to think of specific examples that support your answers because they will serve as evidence that you are on the right path or make the case for some necessary adjustments.

- To what extent have you relied on "carrots and sticks" to gain compliance from those in your leadership sphere?
- How have carrots and sticks fallen short? What were the consequences?

• What's the difference when you're doing something because it is important to you (i.e., you want to) versus when you are conforming to the demands of others (i.e., you have to)? How does the difference impact your commitment, energy level, and focus?

• To what extent have you connected your personal why to your present work? Have there been times in your life when this linkage was clearer?

• How would you rank the level of commitment from your current group of coworkers? What is the basis for your answer?

• Is a lack of commitment interfering with your team's ability to accomplish its mission?

action items

After reflecting on the questions above, choose one or more of the action items below to place on your to-do list this week or this month. Work through the list to gain insight about yourself and others, and allow that insight to inform your practices at work. If your initial attempts at having some of these conversations don't go well, keep trying; however, try not to come across as intrusive.

· Have a series of conversations with the members of your team with a goal of trying to understand what makes their work meaningful to them. In other words, try to discover their personal why. Recognize that this may not be easy for some people to articulate, so gently ask a series of questions that allow them to offer their reasons in their answers. Be patient and listen.

· In a more casual setting, ask coworkers or friends, "If you could have any job in the world, what would it be and why?" Encourage people to go deeper than some of the typical answers like rock star, professional athlete, or lottery winner. Sincere responses will help you understand what really drives a person.

· Ask the members of your team what prevents them from doing their best work. Their answers will give you a sense of what's most important as they begin to list things that interfere with their priorities.

· Invite honest feedback on how well you're demonstrating your commitment to the mission and your team. If you don't like what you hear, don't attack the messenger! Doing so would greatly reduce the likelihood that people will be willing to give you valuable feedback in the future.

additional reading

Why We Do What We Do: Understanding Self-Motivation, Edward Deci, Penguin Books, 1995.

Drive: The Surprising Truth About What Motivates Us, Daniel Pink, Riverhead Books, 2009.

The Search for God and Guinness: A Biography of the Beer that Changed the World, Stephen Mansfield, 2009.

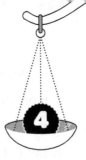

who is on your island?

the power of collaboration

A FEW YEARS AGO, my wife and I enjoyed two perfect weeks in Italy. We began in Rome, where our hotel was in the shadow of the Pantheon, explored the Tuscan countryside in a 1966 Fiat 500, and concluded our visit by floating the canals of Venice, where we discovered the beauty of Murano glass.

Anyone who isn't familiar with these exquisite pieces of art should search for online images of the bold, delicate, and imaginative glass objects. Seeing these incredible artisans at work really got me thinking about how this art form[1] advanced over the centuries on a small island about a mile north of Venice.

The story began more than a thousand years ago but took a defining turn in 1291 CE, when the Great Council of Venice banned all glassblowing furnaces in the city after a series of fires in the densely populated community.[2] Fortunately, the city fathers recognized the economic importance of this industry, so they designated the less-

---

1 *Venier, The History of Glass in Murano*, available at http://www.vetreriavenier.com/en/glassmaker/history-of-glass-murano-venice (Accessed January 10, 2021).

2-3 *History of Murano Glass*, available at https://www.glassofvenice.com/murano_glass_history.php (Accessed April 6, 2021).

than-one-mile-wide island of Murano to be the new epicenter of glassblowing—and it remains so more than 700 years later.

Artist and scientist Angelo Barovier worked on the island during the 15th century. Through alchemy (a precursor to chemistry), he discovered how to make very refined glass as clear as rock crystal.[3] Soon, nearly everyone on the island had learned and was using the technique. The 16th century is considered the golden age of glasswork, as the artists of Murano began to create with filigrana a reticello—a filigree pattern in subtle, intricate nets. This novel form was soon trending in the royal courts of Europe, with practically every aristocrat and well-to-do person embracing this new status symbol. Meanwhile, most of the glassblowers on Murano knew the techniques associated with the new style and improved upon them. An eruption of shapes and colors arrived in the 18th century, and to this day, the Murano artists continue to push the creative envelope.

The reason this art form has evolved and thrived for so long in such a small place is collaboration. The glassblowers continue to be a close-knit community. A few may be driven to outdo the other shops, but whatever the motive, Murano remains a place for unbridled creativity fueled by a collective desire for excellence.

No matter our location—Murano, Montmarte, or Silicon Valley—we learn from each other. Most present-day leaders agree and declare collaboration to be a building block of their organization. Unfortunately, it's much easier to say that we value collaboration than to actually do it. Yet, leaders must recognize barriers to the free exchange of ideas and overcome them with actions that encourage people to leverage the insights of others to make better decisions and get more done.

Barriers to Collaboration

Researchers Lynda Gratton and Tamara Erickson studied the reasons for collaboration, as well as what gets in the way.[4] Interestingly, the two lists were almost identical. The first driving factor for collaboration is team size. Traditionally, teams rarely had more than 20 members. Smaller teams are consistent with Amazon CEO and founder Jeff Bezos' two-pizza rule.[5] He famously limits meeting attendance—and team size—to the number of people who can be fed with two pizzas.

The same isn't true for all organizations, though.

Teams are often larger now because of the complexity of projects and a desire for input from a wide array of subject matter experts and stakeholders. These people often are scattered around the world, working on different aspects of important projects. It doesn't take a business professor to recognize that, as more people become involved, it's more difficult to get everyone talking, much less cooperating.

4 Lynda Gratton and Tamara J. Erickson. "8 Ways to Build Collaborative Teams." *Harvard Business Review*, vol. 85, no. 11, November 2007, pp. 100-109.

5 Aine Cain, "Jeff Bezos's productivity tip? The two-pizza rule: The trick helps Amazon's founder keep his meetings productive and useful," *Inc.*, June 2014, available at https://www.inc.com/business-insider/jeff-bezos-productivity-tip-two-pizza-rule.html (Accessed January 16, 2021).

The next factor—people working virtually—became reality for many people in 2020 as most organizations closed or dramatically cut staffing in their offices to reduce the spread of the coronavirus. Teammates who regularly met face to face for staff meetings or project updates—and consistently found time to catch up on personal matters over lunch or coffee—now had to meet virtually.

We are all grateful for this technology, but there is plenty of frustration with it, as well. Many quickly tired of the constant competition for bandwidth on home Wi-Fi networks, background noise and distractions, and a general lack of spontaneity. Virtual meetings somehow make us wearier, as well, so a new body of knowledge has emerged to help us combat Zoom fatigue. However, even when the pandemic is behind us, these challenges are not likely to go away. With tech giants Google, Facebook, and Twitter announcing that work-from-home initiatives will last well beyond the pandemic's end and surveys suggesting that one in six American workers will continue to telework,[6] the challenges of remote work are certain to remain.

As organizations have rightly focused on diversity and including different perspectives to spark creativity and innovation, we see new challenges for communication and collaboration. Like it or not, when people perceive differences in themselves and others, they are often hesitant to share ideas or engage in robust debate. Truth is, the very things organizations need—openness to new ideas, access to

---

6 Derek Thompson, "The workforce is about to change dramatically: Three predictions for what the future might look like," *The Atlantic*, August 6, 2020, available at https://www.theatlantic.com/ideas/archive/2020/08/just-small-shift-remote-work-could-change-everything/614980/ (Accessed January 16, 2021).

different perspectives, and creative thinking—are tied to people who don't know one another very well.

Technology and complexity of work have risen sharply, as have the educational levels and specializations of team members. In some cases, these subject matter experts seem to speak different languages, making it hard for team members who don't understand that specialized language.

I have some personal experience with this one. By any measure, I am a highly educated person with a terminal degree and a boatload of training over the course of my career. Still, I regularly find myself in meetings with software engineers and clueless as to what they're talking about. Try as I may, their vocabularies and processes are foreign to me. Fortunately, a few of the engineers diligently and patiently translate terms and concepts, but it slows us down and remains an ongoing challenge.

Despite these threats to collaboration, leaders must find ways to get the best ideas on the table. It can be difficult, but collaboration is a critical component of creativity, innovation, and process improvement. Simply put, performance can't improve without it.

Creating a Culture of Collaboration

Whether a team effectively collaborates is largely determined by the leader. What the leader says and, more importantly, what the leader does often determines how freely the team shares ideas and works together to solve the most pressing problems. The following ideas should guide how you create a culture of collaboration for your organization.

No man is an island. English poet John Donne recognized the interconnectedness of humanity nearly 400 years ago with this frequently quoted line.[7] We confronted this truth during the coronavirus pandemic, as we suffered through the social isolation that resulted from the need to distance ourselves from others. Sadly, the poem's other famous stanza that asks "for whom the bell tolls" was heartbreakingly real for way too many. If nothing else, the experience highlights the importance of relationships in a way that none of us can soon forget.

> Collaboration recognizes that no one can ever
> have all the answers.

Real trouble awaits any leader—and their team—who can't embrace this foundational premise and become open to the ideas of others. A great example of collaboration across a wide array of stakeholders and experts played out successfully was the 2018 rescue of the soccer team from the rapidly flooding cave in Thailand.[8] The

---

7 Merton, Thomas. *No Man Is an Island.* New York: Harcourt Brace Jovanovich, 1978.

8 Radhika Viswanthan, "The rescue of the 12 Thai boys who were trapped in a cave, explained," *Vox.com*, July 19, 2018, available at https://www.vox.com/science-and-health/2018/7/5/17532464/thai-soccer-team-cave-rescue-diving-monsoon (Accessed January 15, 2021).

17-day campaign to rescue the boys and their coach involved hundreds of experts and highly skilled operators.

Each person there was a top performer in his or her respective field; however, success hinged on their willingness to listen and ultimately cede control to others. An example was set when a lesser-known engineer suggested placing large pipes high on the mountainside above the cave to divert the rushing water. Other more senior engineers or Thai naval operators could have tried to force another solution, but they didn't. They flexed, the idea worked, and the boys were saved.

Complexity often calls for close cooperation between a wide array of stakeholders and experts from different departments—even different organizations. The presence of a central authority or project manager makes sense, but the benefits of collaboration disappear when leaders are unwilling to listen and delegate responsibility. Success means giving up control and resisting the urge to micromanage, even when the stakes are incredibly high. A leader's willingness to do this is often rooted in how well you know and trust your colleagues to get the job done.

Have no strangers on your island. As a boy, I regularly visited my grandparents in a small town in southern Missouri. No one locked their doors and people would stop by unannounced and visit for hours on front porches. My grandparents seemed to know everyone, as they exchanged waves with people in passing cars and frequently stopped to talk at length with fellow shoppers during trips to the grocery (yes, there was only one in town).

I believe this friendly, small-town atmosphere should be the cultural goal for even large enterprises. It should be a place where people are known and appreciated, spontaneous conversations are frequent and comfortable, and everyone looks out for their neighbor. This can happen in either structured or informal ways. Both can work and should begin early, eventually becoming embedded in the daily rhythms of work.

This work begins during the recruiting process and continues even if the employee moves on to other opportunities. My son was recruited to join a particular public defender's office after law school, and the senior attorney conducting the interview invited him to contact other young attorneys who had passed through that office on their career journey. Everyone he called was generous with their time, forthcoming with information, and incredibly gracious in conversation. Those interactions gave him a good sense for the type of people with whom he would be working and collaborating.

A manager should invest time to orient a new employee, arrange for conversations with key colleagues and stakeholders, and invite ideas and observations. Designating a peer sponsor is also helpful; however, choose carefully, so as not to partner a disgruntled stayer with an enthusiastic new recruit. While HR might create the process and training that allows all of this to occur, part of the responsibility of onboarding new employees falls to their team.

Along the way, leaders should facilitate opportunities for co-workers to get to know one another in social settings, as well. Some, like the military's Hail and Farewell ceremonies, are based on long-standing traditions and are fairly formal. At the other end of the spectrum are the impromptu happy hours or fun events, like team bowling or golf outings. All of these approaches can work but resist the temptation to create forced events that people may not enjoy yet feel required to attend.

Consider this example of regular gatherings that did wonders for a nonprofit organization. It was simple—each month, the large team sat down for a luncheon to celebrate everyone who had a birthday during that month. These celebrations occasionally were held off site at a restaurant, but usually, food was delivered or people brought in a favorite dish to share. But more than the food, the point was that people had time and space to interact informally and get to know each other. Most importantly, each person had to share their sincere appreciation for the birthday boy or girl. These words let the celebrants know they are a valuable part of the team, and these inexpensive events quickly became quite popular.

Of course, there are structured ways to get to know your team members and others in the enterprise. One of the best involves using a valid and reliable psychometric—a personality assessment—to understand your coworkers' personalities and learn how to best work with them.

There are many good assessments on the market, but my personal favorite is the SDI 2.0. It focuses on relationships and how to forge better dialogue. It most certainly increases self-awareness, as well, and the easy-to-remember colors and simple, common language help with application. More about SDI 2.0 is available online at www.CoreStrengths.com.

Build bridges to other islands. I was surprised to learn during our visit that Venice is built on a series of 120 small islands connected by bridges and canals. These points of connection are critical to its existence. Likewise, cross-functional collaboration can't occur unless there are points of connection between people who focus on different aspects of the work.

One of the best ways to build relational bridges is to identify mutual interests, much like we do when making personal friends. Mutual interests seem to be an instinctual draw. Have you ever been at a large event with hundreds of strangers, yet somehow you stumble across someone from your hometown or who graduated from the same university as you? You're immediately energized as you dive into discovering what else you may have in common. Whether it's a cause, your interest in restoring antique cars, or that you both cheer for the same sports team, a common interest often opens the door to friendship.

Research supports this desire to bond with people we deem to be like us. However, social psychologist Hans Alves from the University of Cologne in Germany[9] found that rare common interests inspire stronger connections. In other words, the fact that two people are employed by the same global corporation creates a base level of

9 Hans Alves, "Sharing Rare Attitudes Attracts," *Personality and Social Psychology Bulletin*, vol. 44, no. 8, 2018, pp. 1270-1283.

connection. The fact that two people are involved in similar projects—like the implementation of new accounting software in their respective divisions or that both are interested in harnessing the same type of nano technology—takes the potential to a much higher level. In fact, the more obscure the common interest, the stronger the pull to form a relationship.

One way, then, for leaders to expand their network and build bridges to people elsewhere in the organization is to seek out people with mutual interests. This will certainly be easier for outgoing people, but all leaders, no matter how they are wired, need to become comfortable at bridge building. Some organizations or industries form interest groups to ease the process of finding like-minded people. If these affinity groups don't exist in your organization, start one!

Leaders strengthen the bridges they have built by creating win-win interactions. Very few of us would happily collaborate with a colleague who takes credit for our work or readily "throws us under the bus" with executive sponsors when a shared endeavor isn't successful. Only a glutton for punishment would continue a voluntary alliance with that exploiter.

Strong bridges of collaboration are only possible when all involved feel they are benefitting from the relationship. Some people simply want to feel they are helping, while others are out to deploy their hard-earned expertise in a forum of peers (i.e., academic conferences), and still others purely want to help the team win. Whatever their motivation, the people involved need to benefit from the collaboration.

Knowing what's important to your team members is the best way to make sure they are getting what they need. Harvard Business School professor Francesca Gino has an effective activity[10] she does with her MBA students: Working in pairs, students are asked to divide an orange. Seems pretty straightforward for the best and brightest MBA students, right? The twist is that each student is provided with their reason for wanting part of the orange—one student wants the orange to make juice; the other needs the peel for baking—but the reason is unknown to their partner. If they discover the other's unique needs, it's easy to create a solution that works for both. If they don't make the effort to learn what matters to the other person, they might resort to cutting the orange in half or perhaps even fighting over the entire orange.

Leaders learn the needs of others by asking questions that invite detailed answers and then carefully listening to what they say. Collaboration is a two-way street, so leaders must be open and transparent about what they're after. Playing one's cards close to the vest might work in poker, but not in collaboration.

Transparency inspires trust.

---

10 Francesca Gino, "Cracking the Code on Sustained Collaboration," *Harvard Business Review*, November-December 2019, pp. 1-11.

Hidden agendas and keeping secrets are like removing planks from the bridges you're trying to build.

Don't be a Gilligan. Consider Gilligan, the bumbling but lovable character played by Bob Denver in the 1960s television comedy, *Gilligan's Island*. Even younger readers have probably seen at least a few of the 94 episodes in syndication and know the standard storyline. The seven shipwrecked castaways are always working to escape the remote island, yet every valiant attempt is somehow foiled, often by one of Gilligan's silly mistakes.

Leaders can inadvertently do silly things that inhibit collaboration, so this might be a good time to do a personal after-action review of your last few meetings or interactions with members of your team. Do you cut people off in midsentence? Have you rejected a colleague's idea in a way that caused them to shut down? When you ask for input, does your team jump in with ideas or do you hear crickets? In the reflection questions that follow, dig deep to identify behaviors that you may need to change in order to have greater team collaboration.

Leaders should be excellent role models of effective collaboration. Put simply, your people should see you in action. It's critical that your colleagues and teammates see you freely exchanging ideas and information—without you doing all the talking. Make yourself visible, ask questions, and be patient as people share their ideas. Above all, thank people when they make the effort to add value.

reflection

Spend as much time as needed to answer the following questions about whether you are modeling collaboration. Try to think of specific examples that support your answers because they will show you are on the right path or make the case for some adjustments.

- How do you exhibit curiosity at work ? Are you sincerely interested in what your colleagues are working on? How would they know? There will be more on curiosity in a later chapter, as well.

- What makes you a good listener? Do you give your full attention to the person speaking or do you mentally wander? Do you interrupt? How often do people seek you out to share a new idea or update you on a project?

- In team meetings, do you usually know what you want to do or are you truly open to the team's ideas? Do you allow adequate time for exploration or brainstorming?

- How often do you ask questions of colleagues, customers, or team members—not to put people on the spot, but to learn from them?

- Is it safe for members of your team to respectfully disagree with you? How comfortable are you with dissent?

Have you made comments in a meeting that seemed to shut down discussion?

- When was the last time you proactively reached out to a colleague in another department? How engaged are you with other departments when there's no impending dead-line or required action?

- When is the last time you met with a colleague or team member over lunch or coffee—or had a virtual meeting—to explore what matters most to them?

Your honest answers to these questions speak loudly about your willingness to collaborate and whether you're modeling collaborative behaviors. If you think you can do better in any area, develop a spe-cific action plan to drive your growth. The action items below will help you get started.

action items

After reflecting on the questions above, choose one or more of the action items below to place on your to-do list this week or this month. Work through the list to refine best practices that work for you. If you are consistent and make these actions habits, you will see better results.

- Call two colleagues in other departments or areas of the business to ask about their most important projects. Offer help or ideas, if appropriate.

- Ask two members of your team to identify things that could be done differently in order to improve a process or outcome. Patiently listen and don't push back.

- At your next team meeting, spend at least 10 minutes brainstorming possible approaches to a new initiative or improvements to an existing process. Remember, brainstorming is meant to create a forum for all ideas—even ones that may not work.

- Let your manager know that you want to become a more collaborative leader and model this skill for others. Invite his/her feedback.

- Ask a friend for advice. Collaboration involves a willingness to receive input.

As you work through these action items, consider how it felt to try something new and whether this behavior was positively received by others. If you have found something that works, keep it up. If the new behavior was difficult or felt awkward, keep working at it until it becomes a natural part of the way you interact with others.

additional reading

Think Again: The Power of Knowing What You Don't Know, Adam Grant, Viking Books, 2021.

Leading from Anywhere: The Essential Guide to Managing Remote Teams, David Burkus, Houghton Mifflin Harcourt Publishing Company, 2021.

"Eight Ways to Build Collaborative Teams", Lynda Gratton and Tamara J. Erickson, *Harvard Business Review*, November 2007, pp. 100-109.

"Cracking the Code of Sustained Collaboration: Six New Tools for Training People to Work Better Together", Francesca Gino, *Harvard Business Review*, November-December 2019, pp. 1-11.

words matter

so choose them carefully

WORDS MATTER—AT LEAST when it comes to markets. Elon Musk sent the price of bitcoin soaring by 20% with just a few keystrokes in his Twitter account.[1] The billionaire entrepreneur's fast fingers have gotten him in hot water with the Securities and Exchange Commission (SEC) more than once, but I'm skeptical that one of the richest men in the world would allow himself to be muzzled.

Musk isn't alone.

No one is more famous (or infamous, depending on your political persuasion) than Donald Trump. The former U.S. president did not confine his exaggerated rhetoric to Twitter. His fiery speech before a throng of passionate supporters, some of whom later stormed the U.S. Capitol, prompted his second impeachment. His defenders argue that Trump was simply exercising his right to free speech, while his detractors contend that his provocative words were incendiary.

1   Billy Bambrough. "Tesla CEO Elon Musk just sent Bitcoin sharply higher, boosting its price over 20%." *Forbes*, January 29, 2021, available at https://www.forbes.com/sites/ billybambrough/2021/01/29/elon-musk-just-sent-bitcoin-sharply-higher-boosting-its-price-almost-20/?sh=20a589f6b14e (Accessed 10 February 2021).

These examples and many others make for juicy media headlines, but the power of words also shows up in less conspicuous ways. In an interview with *Scientific American*, cognitive scientist Lera Boroditsky of the University of California, San Diego, explained how word choice can alter our perception of the world.[2] In one example, she suggested that when a supermarket promotes ground beef as 80% lean, it might give the impression it is healthier than a package that is 20% fat. In reality, it's the same meat, although shopper behavior just might be influenced by the words used to describe it.

Words and how we use them have, of course, been widely studied by scholars who make their living producing academic papers. One time-tested example is the Sapir-Whorf hypothesis. First advanced by Edward Sapir (1884-1939) and his student, Benjamin Whorf (1897-1941), nearly 100 years ago, the theory suggests that language structure influences how people perceive their world. Some have called it the theory of relativity for linguistics.[3]

The big idea of this theory and its slightly softer version, Neo-Whorfianism, is that if a language doesn't have a word to describe something, then a person who speaks that language has no way to conceptualize that thing. As with any academic theory, there is scholarly debate about its validity. In this case, critics argue that

---

2   Dina Fine Maron. "Why words matter: What cognitive science says about prohibiting certain terms." *Scientific American*, December 19, 2017, available at https://www.scientificamerican.com/article/why-words-matter-what-cognitive-science-says-about-prohibiting-certain-terms/ (Accessed 10 February 2021).

3   Richard Nordquist. "The Sapir-Whorf hypothesis linguistic theory." ThoughtCo., July 3, 2019, available at https://www.thoughtco.com/sapir-whorf-hypothesis-1691924 (Accessed 10 February 2021).

language does not necessarily limit a human's ability to reason and feel emotion; however, it certainly helps a person do those things.

So, what's the connection with leading people and getting stuff done in your organization? The way you use words affects how people feel about themselves, the mission, their coworkers, and the organization. Moreover, when pursuing goals, words provide fuel for action.

> **Words and the emotions they invoke are often the bridge between people and performance.**

In some cases, words are like shots of adrenaline that provide energy to continue the fight. In this vein, sports commentators have attempted to rank the all-time best halftime locker room speeches.[4] Among the most popular is Tim Tebow's emotional message to his Florida teammates during the 2009 BCS Championship game. A fierce first-half battle had left Florida and top-ranked Oklahoma tied, 7-7. Tebow, the 2007 Heisman Trophy winner and a senior leader at quarterback, gathered the Gators around him in a circle at halftime and shouted: "We've got 30 minutes for the rest of our lives—30 minutes for the rest of our lives! ... Look at me! Look at me! We've got 30 minutes for the rest of our lives!"

Florida went on to win, 24-14, in front of a Dolphin Stadium record crowd of nearly 80,000 fans.[5]

---

4 *USA TODAY* Sports. "What are the best locker room speeches of all time?" *USA TODAY*, December 17, 2012, available at https://www.usatoday.com/story/gameon/2012/12/17/best-locker-room-speeches/1775727/ Accessed 11 February 2021).

5 ESPN College Sports

If you haven't seen it, I encourage you to search for the video. By the end, Tebow will have you wanting to strap on a helmet and pads and go hit someone. Just to be clear, though (and to avoid potential legal consequences), that's not acceptable in most workplaces.

Words don't have to be delivered in fiery fashion to be effective. The American tradition of peacefully transferring power from one administration to the next includes the outgoing president leaving a handwritten note for his successor in the Oval Office.

Bill Clinton often becomes emotional when asked about the note he received from George H.W. Bush. Although they came from different political parties, represented different ideologies, and had just completed a hard-fought election, former President Bush's letter was sincere, kind, and encouraging. Most importantly, it was a reminder of the two men's shared commitment to the good of the country. Later, perhaps as a result of this traditional letter, they became close friends who joined forces in many humanitarian projects.

Of course, words can also do great harm. Michelle Carter is a Massachusetts woman convicted of involuntary manslaughter for encouraging her 18-year-old boyfriend, Conrad Roy III, to commit suicide in a series of text messages and telephone calls.[6] Roy, who suffered from depression, eventually succumbed to Carter's verbal pressure and killed himself by inhaling fumes from a generator he

---

6 Gabrielle Bruney. "Michelle Carter was convicted of encouraging her boyfriend to kill himself. Here's what happened next." *Esquire*, October 7, 2019, https://www.esquire.com/entertainment/tv/a28339149/where-michelle-carter-is-now-jail-i-love-you-now-die-true-story/ (Accessed 11 February 2021).

had placed in his car. Carter was only 17 when she used words to create this devastating outcome.

When you recognize the incredible power of words, it's incumbent to examine how you use them. The following section is a good place to start. As you read, make notes in the margin to reflect the key people in your life and how you use your words with them. If you don't like what you see, commit to using your words more effectively in the future.

Harsh Words Sting and Stick

My high school memories are few, but I distinctly recall a toasty spring afternoon on a rival school's baseball field, the words that were said, and how I felt in response. By no means was I the best player on the team, but I was fast. And, as the fastest player on our team, I was often called on to steal a base or pinch-run for a slower teammate. The latter was what got me off the bench and into the game on this particular afternoon.

Our catcher, a husky kid known as Bobo, hit a two-out single up the middle and waddled to first base. Since we were down by a run and Bobo's 40-yard dash time was measured with an hourglass, the coach put me in to pinch run. The next batter hit a shot to right-center and I easily went from first to third. So, here we were, late in the game, runners on the corners with two outs. The third-base coach came over and whispered in my ear: "Big lead. Go on contact."

I could certainly follow directions, so I started to take big side-steps toward home plate while keeping my eyes on the pitcher and the ball in his hand. After a couple of called balls, I started to become a bit more daring with my lead. Before I could respond, the pitcher whirled around and threw a knee-high strike—to the third baseman. Caught in a rundown, the play and the inning quickly ended with my shame-filled shuffle to the visitors' dugout, which just so happened to be a few feet behind where the embarrassing incident had occurred.

Our coach wasted no time in throwing some choice words my way: "Patterson, you idiot! I could have left Bobo in the game to get picked off. Give me 10 laps!" Laps? During a game? At someone else's field? He was harsh, but he had never issued that sort of degrading punishment.

By the time I finished running, the game had long concluded (we lost) and my team was on the bus. Everyone was silent when I climbed in and took my seat in the second row right behind the coach. It was clear that he was still angry—in part because the vein in his neck was pulsating like a boa constrictor trying to swallow its prey—but also because he didn't swivel around in his seat or even attempt to create a teaching moment during the ride home, although there was abundant opportunity.

I loved baseball, but I didn't go out for the team the next year. It's not that I could have had a pro career, and one might call me weak for not going back, but I just moved on. All of the wind was out of my sails—at least when it came to high school baseball.

The amazing thing about this 45-year-old story is that every detail is true, and I remember it like it was yesterday. I recall the words that were said, the feeling of the sweat dripping down the back of my neck as I ran those laps, and the dejection that filled the bus during the ride home.

Fortunately, things have changed. Most coaches know not to berate students in front of their peers and, generally speaking, we are more civil in the way we treat kids. Neither would most organizations tolerate such abusive outbursts from managers.

The point is that my coach's harsh words, spoken in a heated moment, remain fresh in my memory. Why?

Science suggests it has something to do with how our brains are wired and who we are. Clifford Nass, a professor of communication at Stanford University, says that even people with a generally rosy view of the world find it much easier to recall bad memories than good ones.[7] In part, that's because we tend to think more about the negative, so the brain works harder to process that information. Turns out, the bad memories that become so detail rich and easy to recall are not reserved for traumatic events—anything perceived as negative seems to be stickier.

If we were able to take an MRI of your brain, we would instantly see the neural changes created when you see or hear negatives words. You would also experience a sudden release of stress-produc-

7 Alina Tugend. Praise is fleeting, but brickbats we recall." *The New York Times*, May 23, 2012, available at available at https://www.nytimes.com/2012/03/24/your-money/why-people-remember-negative-events-more-than-positive-ones.html (Accessed 12 February 2021).

ing hormones and neurotransmitters.[8] The part of the brain most active in the secretion of these chemicals is the amygdala, which also affects how we process information and respond to threatening situations. Daniel Goleman, the psychologist who popularized emotional intelligence (EQ), coined the phrase "amygdala hijacking" to describe how a person may illogically overreact to a stressful or fear-inducing situation.[9]

Beyond MRI machines and brain chemicals, researchers like Ray Baumeister, a professor of social psychology at Florida State University, and his colleagues, suggest that it is fundamental to our human nature to remember the bad more clearly than the good. In their classic article "Bad is Stronger than Good", published in *The Review of General Psychology* in 2001, they put it plainly: "Bad emotions, bad parents, and bad feedback have more impact than good ones."[10] They offer a simple example from the empirical research: Most people are more upset about losing $50 than they are excited when they win $50. Likewise, people are often more upset by criticism than they are encouraged by praise. It's the bad stuff that seems to stick with us.

Don't take this as a suggestion that leaders shouldn't offer constructive feedback that has some critical components. I deserved no

---

8 A. Talarovicova, L. Krskova & A. Kiss. "Some assessments of the amygdala role in suprahypothalamic neuroendocrine regulation: A minireview." *Endocrine Regul.*, November 2007; 41(4). Pp. 155-162.

9 Daniel Goleman. *Emotional Intelligence: Why it Can Matter More than IQ.* NY: Bantom Books, 2005.

10 Roy F. Baumeister, Ellen Bratslavsky, Catrin Finkenauer, and Kathleen D. Vohs. "Bad Is Stronger than Good." *Review of General Psychology*, no. 4 (December 2001): 323–70. https://doi.org/10.1037/1089-2680.5.4.323. P. 328.

applause when my poor base-running caused my team to lose the game; therefore, I needed feedback that would help me learn and do better next time. Had I received that kind of feedback, my baseball career just might have taken a different path.

Honest but Kind

In a chapter on words, honest and kind are two that might not seem to go together. But there are numerous examples of where it happens—or should happen—every day. It happens to me at least once per year during my annual physical exam. After looking me over and reading my lab results, my physician will sit down on that little rolling stool that seems to have a place in every exam room to ask, "How are you doing with your exercise routine?" Like clock-work, that question is followed by a mini lecture about how I would benefit from losing a few pounds and how losing a few pounds would be a lot easier if I cut back on the carbs and sugar. The doctor goes on to tell me the risks for a guy my age if I don't eat right, exercise, and keep my weight down. That's truth.

When it's over, I'm not angry at my doctor. I need to hear that honest feedback, and it's his job to give it to me. It's my job to respond to the truth. And I'm trying, so don't judge.

Leaders unwilling to speak the truth are not doing their jobs. Some withhold helpful information in order to avoid even the small-est risk of confrontation, while others allow the pendulum to swing so sharply in the other direction that they deliver stinging rebukes that are resented by the recipients and completely miss the mark. Why? It's their perceived inability to balance honesty with kindness.

If you pause for a moment, you can probably identify certain people in your life who can tell you anything—and you will listen. They speak truth and you're grateful to the point that you turn to them in the most difficult moments of life for guidance. How did that person earn that position of trust? Why will you listen to them but resent similar feedback from others? The answer often lies within your assumptions about their intentions.

I do not resent or resist the guidance of my doctor because, presumably, his words and actions are intended for my good. When he tells me to cut back on the cookies, I don't immediately label him a sadistic man who enjoys seeing me suffer. Instead, I believe he has my best interests at heart, he is credible to speak on matters related to health and nutrition, and I have had a series of positive interactions with him over the years.

Good intentions, credibility, and relationship history allow you to be honest with people. In some cases, you can put these important credentials to work immediately; other times, you'll need some time to demonstrate their validity. Sometimes, two out of three will be enough to gain people's attention. Rarely, however, will only one of the three be enough to build that bridge of trust. It's also true that if one of the three is in horrible shape, you'll probably not get there either.

Some people more easily check these boxes than others. It just comes with their territory. Most of us, however, must prove that we have the credentials to be heard. The paragraphs that follow contain some simple tips that you can apply immediately when you want to be honest with people.

A basic concern of many people relates to your intentions. Are you a friend or foe? This instinct likely developed many generations ago, when letting the wrong person inside your camp or the walls of your city might get you killed or conquered. That instinct still exists today for most people. So, how do we pass muster with someone's intention detector? The easiest way is to simply and sincerely state your intentions early-on in a difficult conversation.

There are no magic words, but a few simple examples might be useful:

- "I'm concerned about you/your... Can I provide some feedback?"
- "I've learned a few things the hard way... Can I share some of those lessons so that you won't have the same experience?"
- "It seems you could use some help. Can I offer some advice?"
- "I really want you to succeed... Would you mind if I gave you some ideas on how you can get there?
- "I don't want to see you get hurt, so..."

Notice two things about each of the examples. The object of concern is the welfare of the other person, not you. Notice that none of the examples began with:

- "I really need to get this off my chest..."
- "You embarrassed me out there, so I'm going to let you have it!"
- "Your dumb decisions are costing me a lot of money."

It's difficult to convey good intentions toward another person when you're talking about yourself.

Stated or implied in each of these examples is a valuable message for the other person—if they will listen. They can avoid a hardship or negative consequence, become more proficient at a task, solve a problem, or achieve a goal. Who in their right mind wouldn't accept that sort of gift?

Another aspect that usually helps is that you are asking for permission to share your truth. In hierarchical structures like the military, a person of lesser rank might ask "permission to speak freely" before addressing a superior officer. I don't recall hearing anyone really say that when I was in the Army, but the principle holds true. It is a sign of respect for the other person to ask permission to speak candidly. Even if you're dealing with a direct report, it's a sign of respect to ask if they are open to receiving feedback.

Next is credibility. Do you know what you're talking about? My physician completed medical school, is licensed to practice medicine in the state of California, and has a bustling practice. This all suggests that he is qualified to speak to me about my health. Would I accept financial advice from him? Spiritual direction? Advice on rebuilding a carburetor? Probably not, without knowing if he is accredited in those areas.

Sometimes, your position provides a certain degree of credibility. However, in "flatter" organizations where technical expertise is often key in solving complex problems, it's important to acknowledge one's limitations. Humility goes a long way and can even build credibility. Often, humbly stating what you don't know is a good place to start an honest conversation.

Your history with a person also affects whether you will accept their honesty. Your longevity with parents, spouse, and/or closest friends certainly influences their degree of candor and your willingness to accept it. In fact, anything less than complete honesty from those closest to you could be considered an act of betrayal.

Of course, a pattern of hurt and disappointment can limit what you're willing to hear. You are likely to be cautious around people who have wounded you emotionally, and you should. The same warning bells can also go off around certain coworkers.

The good news is that each interaction with someone is an opportunity to co-create the future and chart a new course. In other words, a rocky start can be mended. It may be necessary to reset expectations, acknowledge and even apologize for past misdeeds, and renew your mutual commitment to respectful and professional discourse. One of the reflection questions at the end of this chapter invites you to take stock of your relational history with key people in your life. If what you discover is displeasing, you can begin making changes that will positively affect the future of your relationships.

No matter how good your relationship with someone, honesty without kindness can feel heartless. It's difficult—even illogical—to imagine that someone I perceive to be cold and callous has my best interest in mind. The combination can lead to a rejection of their message, no matter how important it might be. On the other hand, it's hard not to listen to someone who consistently treats you with kindness.

Kind acts and words typically cost nothing, but they can create lasting value. In case you're struggling with what it means to use kind words, here are some examples that you can easily work into your daily conversations:

- Thank you.
- You're welcome.
- I'm happy for you.
- I really appreciated it when…
- I'm sorry.
- What do you think?
- Your hard work is really paying off.
- I can see you put a lot of thought into this.
- That must have been hard; I'm glad you hung in there.
- That sounds like a good decision.
- How can I help?

- What do you need from me?
- You've accomplished a lot since we last met.
- You're one of the most persistent people I know.
- I can see your progress.

Granted, there's nothing fancy or frilly about these phrases. But just as toddlers struggle with kindness when playing with siblings and friends, we sometimes forget our manners. It's also important to note that kindness is a condition of the heart. Insincerely reciting words from note cards can doom a message from the get-go. Nevertheless, try. Practice makes perfect.

If you believe that kindness somehow equates to weakness—and you would never want to be identified as a weak leader—consider the example of Agnes Bojaxhiu. As a young woman, Agnes left her family and comfortable life, learned a new language, and moved into one of the worst slums the world has ever known. With no support, she had to beg in order to survive—just like the widows, orphans, and lepers she went there to serve. But the strength of her resolve and the magnitude of the mission kept her focused.

Over time, Agnes developed an organization that garnered respect from every corner of the globe, gave her ready access to heads of state, and made her one of the most recognizable people on the planet. Ultimately, Agnes' achievements were recognized with a Nobel Peace Prize, placing her in the company of some of history's greatest statesmen. Agnes passed in 1997, but her life remains synonymous with strength, resilience, and commitment—and the antithesis of weakness. Of course, you probably know her as Mother Teresa.[11]

Now, think back to unkind and envision someone you know who doesn't consistently treat people with respect and dignity. When that person talks, do people listen? If they do, it's probably just to avoid the person's wrath.

Words without kindness might get compliance, but rarely do they lead to commitment to the mission.

Finally, don't confuse kindness with obfuscation—i.e., don't beat around the bush. No one benefits from you confusing the matter with unclear statements that weaken your message. If you have good intentions, credibility, and a solid relational history, just say what you need to say clearly, but with kindness.

So far, our focus has been on leaders and how their overall approach can help engage people in the mission. Leaders also must be able to nimbly adapt their communication style to address the particular needs and even preferences of their audience. The following section will focus on using words that resonate and move people to action.

---

11 Catholic.org. "Mother Teresa of Calcutta." *Catholic Online*, no date, available at https://www.catholic.org/clife/teresa/ (Accessed 15 February 2021).

Words that Resonate

Who is Ulrich Gerhatz? If this was Jeopardy, the TV game-show where contestants' answers must be in question form, you might have won big if the prompt was: The German who many believe to be the most powerful person in classical music. More likely, however, your embarrassing blank stare would be broadcast on national television.

Officially, Gerhatz, is director of the concert department for Steinway & Sons, maker of fine pianos and the frequent choice of the greatest pianists and concert halls worldwide. Unofficially, Gerhatz is the go-to tuner for every top player on the planet.[12] In fact, some of these elite musicians won't step on the stage unless Gerhatz has done the once-over on their instrument. Many of these pianos are valued at well over $100,000 but have relatively short "careers" in the concert hall because newer instruments have a cleaner, brighter sound.

Gerhatz is a master craftsman—methodical and meticulous, but also willing to adjust to the needs of each maestro, who often want pianos set up differently based on their playing style. Some want the keyboard action so light that a feather's touch will create sound; others like to pound out a powerful sound. What makes

---

12 Jasper Rees. "Get me Gerhartz!" *The Guardian*, February 22, 2009, available at https://www.theguardian.com/music/2009/feb/23/ulrich-gerhartz-piano-tuning-bren-del (Accessed February 2021).

Gerhatz special though is his ability to hear how each note resonates. He just knows when the sound is right.

Most people know when something sounds right within the realm of everyday conversations. Some words resonate with us, while others fall flat. This is because of the way each of us is wired and our core values.

Leaders who want to communicate important messages about the mission and inspire people to do their best work must be able to choose words that resonate with each team member. The ability to do this, as we discussed in the chapter about collaboration, is knowing who is on your team, what is important to them, and how they like to communicate. The other critical component is choosing the right words and delivery so that you are hitting the mark and moving people to action.

Let's consider some basic examples.

Your team likely has members who want you to practice the Three Be's of effective communication: Be brief, be brilliant, and be gone! They like the concise, direct approach—devoid of flowery words and meandering stories—because they are laser focused and always busy. They enjoy getting things done and it frustrates them when someone—e.g., the manager who has two-hour staff meetings several times each week—impedes their momentum. Words that resonate for that kind of task-oriented include:

- I'll get right to the point.
- Let's make this brief.

- Here's what needs to happen...
- Why don't you get started right away?
- The bottom line is...
- Let's get going.

In written communication, these people would probably like to see the bottom line (main point) early in the email or memo, so they don't have to search for what's important. Clearly highlighting necessary action and due dates also is greatly appreciated.

If you've correctly assessed their preferred communication style, they will feel understood and even respected because you're communicating efficiently. And because you are honoring their focus, these overachievers generally will perform even better.

Then there are people who like to dig into the details, look at the data, and really think things through. They don't like to be rushed or to make decisions without doing their homework. Words that resonate with this kind of thoughtful, data-driven person might sound like:

- The facts lead us to believe...
- The data supports the decision.
- Here's what we know...
- What's missing?
- Can you help us better understand what we're up against?
- Let's make sure we get this right.

When communicating in writing with these folks, more is often better: more details, more information, more research, more background, more data, and more time to sift through it all and respond.

It's best not to ask these process-driven folks for quick decisions or surprise them with late-breaking news. Assertions should be logical and well grounded.

There will likely be someone on your team who is all about people, relationships and being helpful. Words that appeal to them are likely pro-people, positive, and personal.

Here are some examples:

- I would appreciate your help with...
- I trust you to make the right call.
- How do you feel about...?
- Let's work together on this.
- I'm grateful for...
- What can we do that would best serve?

In conversation or writing, it's probably best not to be critical of others, aggressive, or dismissive of others' concerns. Don't seek to take advantage; instead, always elevate people in your communication.

You're also likely to have one or more folks who totally buy into the team experience. They value collaborative problem solving, want to feel connected and included, and enjoy friendly office banter. These gregarious people tend to be the most frustrated with remote work and distance learning unless there is a committed effort to build community and pave the way for people to positively interact on a regular basis.

Words likely to reach these people include:

- What are your ideas?

- Let's figure it out together.
- I want everyone to have input on this one.
- Can we come to consensus?
- I'm flexible.
- Is there a better way?

It's always good to be perceived as open-minded and open-eared. Whether in word or deed, anytime you fall silent or appear to be holding back, these collaborative folks may become suspicious.

While the nuances of these different communicator types may take time to learn, your big takeaway from this discussion should be that one-size-fits-all approaches do not work. When a leader's words (or actions) suggest a "my way or the highway" attitude toward communicating, some team members—perhaps even the standouts—will choose the open road over a leader who insists on communicating in a manner that doesn't honor their values.

So, how can one know which communication style will work best with each team member? Perhaps more importantly, what words work best with your manager or influential peers? There are plenty of valid and reliable psychometric assessments that help people become more self-aware and, specifically, how they prefer to receive and process information. When these insights are shared with other members of the team, often through group learning experiences, everyone becomes more aware of how their colleagues want and need to communicate. The key is being able to recall this information, as it's very easy to forget under the pressure of deadlines or other stressors.

The SDI 2.0, which we introduced in chapter 4, is my favorite tool for determining how to best use my words. Not only does it measure motives (what drives people) and strengths (how people get things done when working with others), but its proprietary software spells out how to approach others, based on their assessment results. You can even have this program open as you're writing emails or scheduling meetings. Moreover, the publisher of these tools has created a simple and memorable common language that makes it easy for everyone to freely discuss the different personality types and preferred communication styles.

Those without access to sophisticated tools like the SDI 2.0 or other psychometric assessments will have to get to know your team the old-fashioned way: listen to what they say, watch what they do, and ask questions. Oftentimes, something as simple as a sincere question about priorities or preferences can go a long way to building a better relationship.

Strong relationships and teamwork can be developed by following a few simple practices. One is the heartfelt expression of gratitude. Don't thank people for performing mundane duties in a mediocre manner. But, when someone rises above expected effort and sacrifices for the team and mission, or displays resilience in the face of ongoing challenges, it never hurts to offer personal and sincere words of appreciation.

For the budget conscious, gratitude is inexpensive. You don't have to make a grand display of it either. Some might like a few moments in the spotlight with marching bands and a flyover, but most would gladly accept a sincere thank you. This comes easily to leaders who know the value of words. We all forget to say thank you sometimes, but if you regularly struggle to express gratitude, some self-examination may be in order. The ticket to a better working relationship with any colleague is to recognize their value and be able to clearly express why you appreciate them.

Other performance-enhancing uses for words are when you offer encouragement and invite people to dream. Expressing your trust in one's abilities or, at a minimum, recognizing that they're capable of learning and improving, gives hope. Inspiring them to purposefully use their imagination to consider what might be (innovative new products, more efficient processes, healthier teams, the creation of wealth, etc.), suggests that status quo isn't good enough. And sometimes that's what it takes to accomplish the mission—believing that we can do more and be more.

Maybe that's where America's sixth president, John Quincy Adams, developed his famous definition of leadership:

If your actions inspire others to dream more, learn more, do more, and become more, you are a leader.

And since Adams was a former Boylston Professor of Rhetoric and Oratory at his alma mater, Harvard University, it's a pretty good bet that he also placed a high value on words and how people used them. We should, too.

reflection

Spend as much time as needed to answer the following questions about how you are using your words. Try to think of specific examples that support your answers—they will serve as evidence that you are on the right path or that adjustments are needed. And remember, be honest. Self-deception does no one any good—especially you.

- Have you been unduly harsh in choosing your words with a colleague or family member? Is that the conversation you want them to remember 10 years from now? How could you have communicated the same message differently?
- Is there someone who needs a bit more truth from you? How can you deliver this truth in a kind way? If they received and responded to the truth, what would happen?
- Evaluate your relational history with key stakeholders in your professional life. Did an early clash get you off to a rough start? Are you harboring resentment toward a leader or peer because of something he or she said or did?
- How often do you use kind words as your day unfolds? Is it enough? Remember, kindness does not equate to being soft.

- How well do you know your team members' communication preferences? Do you readily adjust your approach to accommodate them? Why or why not?
- Have you caught yourself using a one-size-fits-all approach to communication? How has that worked for you?
- Which coworkers have you sincerely expressed appreciation for or thanked this week?

action items

After reflecting on the questions above, choose one or more of the action items below to place on your to-do list this week or this month. Work through the list to improve your approach with people and develop best practices. If you are consistent and habitual in these practices, results will be obvious in your relationships with people and their performance.

- If you have been unduly harsh with a colleague or family member, apologize. Explain that you should have conveyed your message differently and that you will do better next time.
- If you have been slow to give constructive feedback to a team member or have ignored an issue that should be addressed, set aside time for that difficult conversation this

week. Be honest, but kind, and consider how you might shape your delivery to communicate in the right style.

• As you hold meetings, write emails, and send instant messages, consider the recipient and what's most important to them. Consider whether you need to tweak your communication style to find their sweet spot.

• Say something kind to someone each day for an entire week.

• Sincerely express your gratitude to someone in your organization each day for an entire week. To be clear, unless you work at a coffee shop, the server at the drive-through window doesn't count.

additional reading

Crucial Conversations: Tools for Talking When the Stakes Are High, Kerry Patterson, Joseph Grenny, Ron McMillan, and Al Switzler, McGraw Hill, 2012.

Radical Candor: Be a Kick-Ass Boss Without Losing Your Humanity, Kim Scott, St. Martin's Press, 2019.

Deep Kindness: A Revolutionary Guide for the Way We Think, Talk, and Act in Kindness, Houston Kraft, Tiller Press, 2020

please, disagree

healthy teams have healthy opposition

SOME PEOPLE SEEM drawn to controversy. The terms "easygoing" or "consensus building" are rarely used to describe them; instead, they are often labeled as opinionated and unyielding—even zealous for their cause. Interestingly, though, some of these people become extraordinary leaders. Against the odds, they achieve great things and are often remembered for their strength, resolve, and vision. The late Margaret Thatcher, the "Iron Lady" of British politics, was one of those people.

British playwright and speechwriter Ronald Miller wrote of his former boss: "Margaret Thatcher evoked extreme feelings. To some, she could do no right; to others, no wrong. Indifference was not an option. She could stir almost physical hostility in normally rational people, while she inspired deathless devotion in others."[1] Perhaps that was necessary to survive as the United Kingdom's first woman prime minister, who inherited an economy struggling with inflation, massive budget deficits, and labor unrest. The need to stand strong

1   Joseph Gregory. "Margaret Thatcher, 'Iron Lady' who set Britain on new course, dies at 87." *The New York Times*, April 8, 1963, available at https://www.nytimes.com/2013/04/09/world/europe/former-prime-minister-margaret-thatcher-of-britain-has-died.html (Accessed February 2021).

against the Soviet Union during some of the darkest days of the Cold War made her job no easier.

Yet, despite calling herself a "conviction politician,"[2] she invited people to disagree with her and to forthrightly state their opinions, even opposing ones. In fact, she in no way wanted to be surrounded by agreeable sycophants. Mrs. Thatcher famously said, "I love argument, I love debate. I don't expect anyone to just sit there and agree with me; that's not their job." She understood the value of healthy opposition and she experienced plenty of it.

Debate, Decide, and Commit

Industry titans have recognized how this mindset can create stronger, more innovative organizations and are working to establish debate, decide, and commit cultures. I have seen firsthand how the 80,000 employees of McKesson Corp. strive to live out this mantra in their daily work of distributing pharmaceuticals, medical supplies, and cutting-edge medical technology. CEO Brian Tyler actively encourages respectful debate, grounded in facts and data, to create the best solution as "…one team going after the same goal together."[3] Tyler believes healthy debate leads to the best decisions.

---

2 Reuters Staff. "Britain's Margaret Thatcher, in her own words." Reuters, April 3, 2013, available at https://www.reuters.com/article/us-britain-thatcher-quotes/britains-margaret-thatcher-in-her-own-words-idUSBRE9370LI20130408 (Accessed February 2021).

3 Bryan Tyler. "Debate, decide, and commit." LinkedIn Blog, available at https://www.linkedin.com/pulse/debate-decide-commit-brian-tyler/?articleId=6593609267243294720 (Accessed February 2021).

So does Jeff Bezos—at least when it comes to the importance of **disagreement**. In his 2016 letter to shareholders, the Amazon founder described his philosophy on making decisions. First, for what he described as lightweight decisions, he encourages people to try ideas that may not succeed. In most cases, decisions are reversible. Second, he argues for speed over certainty by suggesting that you should probably make decisions with about 70% of the information you would like to have. If you wait for all of the information, or even 90%, you're probably moving too slow. And, if the decision turns out to be wrong, correct your course and keep moving.

Third, Bezos proposes a disagree and commit philosophy.[4] With this approach, he encourages colleagues to present and advocate for their ideas despite knowing there may be clear points of disagreement. The "boss" may even disagree, but at some point, everyone on the team—including the boss—must commit and give their all to make the plan successful. By way of example, he described a particular project for Amazon Studios that his team wanted to greenlight. Bezos thought the idea lacked strength and would not interest viewers. Yet, after weighing everyone's input, the group approved the project and fully committed to its success.

Bezos' point is that, if people must convince the boss in order to gain acceptance of their ideas, decision making will be excruciatingly slow. A better goal is to gain commitment from key stakeholders

---

4 Jeff Bezos. "2016 letter to Shareholders." Amazon, April 17, 2017, available at https://www.aboutamazon.com/news/company-news/2016-letter-to-shareholders?tag=wwwinc-com-20 (Accessed February 2021).

after vigorous debate, even if there is no ultimate consensus. Ideally, the process should refine the idea enough to make it worthy of team commitment. It's also important, Bezos notes, that it's not about wearing down the holdouts until they concede and go away to pout. Rather, it's a collective resolve to take action that aligns with the combined wisdom of the group.

Debate, decide, and commit as a cultural norm is intended to prevent the "meeting after the meeting." We've all been there. It's when a subset of the people in the original session gather to discuss how they **really** feel about the decision. It's where frustration with ignorant and unlikable coworkers, the potentially disastrous consequences of pursuing the new approach, and other general, loosely relevant gripes, all bubble over to create a strong brew of discontent.

The people involved in the after-meeting regularly find themselves brainstorming potential workarounds or, worse yet, ways to undermine the new approach to ensure its failure. Ironically, these same people were all-in with the new policy in the earlier meeting. In this regard, they are consistently inconsistent.

My first post-Army, professional job in pharmaceutical sales allowed me to experience this phenomenon firsthand. Because my colleagues and I were field based, working out of our homes to make sales calls on doctors, clinics, and hospitals, we gathered in a hotel conference room each quarter to hear about the company's performance and strategy, learn about our products, and discuss how best to convey that message to our customers. We also were provided new sales collateral and given time to discuss and practice using it.

No doubt, the hardworking people back at HQ would spend weeks creating slide decks and other materials, which the district managers would present. The obvious goal was for everyone to align on tactics that all had agreed would give us the best chance of accomplishing our mission. If the goal was achieved, the sales force would charge back to their respective territories with renewed energy and clarity about how to best engage customers.

Things played out differently for my team. Our manager was old school, hovering somewhere between Alec Baldwin's character in the movie *Glengarry Glen Ross* and the guy who could get you a great deal on a slightly used BMW. Don't get me wrong. He was a fine salesman with a long track record of success. But he had always done it **his** way, using his innate skills and unique methods.

At our quarterly meetings, as predictably as the sun rises, my manager would quickly become frustrated with the official presentation, even though he had spent the previous week meeting with his peers to plan and practice what each would say to their sales teams. Now, in front of his own team, he would garble the message of each new sales aid, becoming increasingly frustrated as he worked through the massive slide deck. Soon, he would cast the new, professionally designed sales collateral to the side. On one memorable occasion, he actually tossed all of the new materials into the trash can. This definite act of defiance left no doubt about his views on the home office's understanding of what actually worked in the field. His grand finale was to migrate to the flip chart and begin an extended lesson on what he believed **would** work and how we should do it **his** way.

More than half of that team were junior military officers who had already experienced a lot in life, so we all enjoyed the show. Other colleagues just a few years out of college were appalled. Most just sat there stunned each time our manager would unleash an expletive-laced tirade about the fools in the home office. Looking back, I realize how miserably these meetings failed to get everyone aligned around the company's mission.

After a half dozen of these district meetings, I was promoted, moved to a different team, and I immediately realized that not all managers in the company operated like my old boss. Not too long after, he was caught in some shenanigan that cost him his job. I went on to become one of the marketing department's product managers, who was charged with preparing and presenting slide decks for district sales meetings. By then, I had learned a few things about inspiring sales teams and was able to provide insight about how shaky commitment toward the mission and methods of the firm could lead to trouble.

The Case for Healthy Opposition[5]

Healthy, intelligent debate and the active discussion of different ideas are critical to getting buy-in on a unified approach.

Failure to productively discuss opposing views can yield devastating results.

Take the case of Asiana Airlines Flight 214, the Boeing 777 that crash-landed on July 6, 2013, at San Francisco International Airport (SFO), killing three people and injuring 187. For that matter, consider the string of aviation accidents involving Korean Air in the 1980s and 1990s. Malcom Gladwell, author of the book *Outliers*, contends that some of those crashes may have been linked to Korea's hierarchical societal structure and cultural norms against questioning authority. This, Gladwell suggests, makes flight crews hesitant to call out potential errors by the captain or other authority figures that could lead to disaster.[6]

Gladwell made the same argument to explain Avianca Flight 52, the crash that killed 73 people on New York's Long Island on Jan. 25, 1990. Even though their fuel supply was running dangerously low, the Colombian crew didn't push back against air traffic

---

5 Much of my thinking on healthy opposition was informed by my extensive work with Core Strengths and our previous book, *Have a Nice Conflict: How to Find Success and Satisfaction in the Most Unlikely Places*, Tim Scudder, Michael Patterson, Kent Mitchell, Jossey-Bass, 2012.

6 Gladwell, Malcolm. *Outliers: The Story of Success*. New York: Little, Brown, and Company, 2008.

controllers' orders to circle John F. Kennedy Airport (JFK) until their turn to land.[7] Could the crew's hesitation to disagree with directions—even though they had contradictory information—have caused so many people to die?

The failure of these well-trained, professional flight crews to speak up is cause for concern among aviation safety experts. Korean Airlines and others have beefed up their training and now require crew members to challenge each other—even more senior officers—on matters of flight safety. Thankfully, these ongoing efforts and advances in technology continue to make commercial aviation one the safest forms of travel—and make me feel a little better each time I board a flight.

But are the same safeguards in place when you hand your financial life over to a bank? Wells Fargo was discovered to have fabricated as many as 3.5 million phony bank and credit card accounts between 2009 and 2015. Furthermore, about 190,000 accounts were hit with bogus fees, and 528,000 customers may have been unknowingly enrolled in online bill pay.[8] Investigators primarily blamed aggressive cross-selling tactics by front-line employees in response to unattainable sales targets.

---

7 Howard, Brian. "Coud Malcolm Gladwell's theory of cockpit culture apply to Asiana crash? *National Geographic*, July 10, 2013, available at https://www.nationalgeographic.com/adventure/article/130709-asiana-flight-214-crash-korean-airlines-culture-outliers (Accessed February 2021).

8 Egan, Matt. "Wells Fargo uncovers up to 1.4 million more fake accounts." *CNN Business*, August 31, 2017, available at https://money.cnn.com/2017/08/31/investing/wells-fargo-fake-accounts/index.html (Accessed February 2021).

Cleaning up hasn't come cheap. Wells Fargo agreed to pay $3 billion in fines to settle cases brought by the U.S. Justice Department.[9] This is in addition to previous fines of $185 million, reimbursing customers for $6.1 million in fees, the $142 million settlement of an old class-action suit, and a nearly $1 billion fine from the Consumer Financial Protection Bureau (CFPB) and the Office of the Comptroller of the Currency (OCC). The biggest hit, although more difficult to measure, was on Wells Fargo's reputation with its customers.

Who's to blame? John Stumpf, former CEO, was personally fined $17.5 million for failure to comply with banking laws and is barred from ever again working in the financial services industry. In total, eight executives were fined for their roles in the illegal activities. Carrie Tolstedt, head of the division most immediately involved with the fraud, faces up to $25 million in personal fines. All told, 5,300 Wells Fargo employees were fired as a result of the fiasco.[10]

Shareholders, regulators, and the public must ask whether this costly mess could have been prevented. Wells Fargo's board of directors concluded in their own investigation that an aggressive sales culture—and intense pressure to meet unrealistic expectations—

---

9 Horsley, Scott. "Wells Fargo paying $3 billion to settle U.S. case over fraudulent customer accounts." NPR, February 21, 2020. Available at https://www.npr.org/2020/02/21/808205303/wells-fargo-paying-3-billion-to-settle-u-s-case-over-illegal-sales-practices (Accessed February 2021).

10 Bayly, Lucy. "Former head of Wells Fargo banned from banking after role in sales scandal." NBC News, January 23, 2020, available at https://www.nbcnews.com/business/business-news/former-head-wells-fargo-banned-banking-after-role-sales-scandal-n1121396 (Accessed February 2021).

pushed employees to act unethically. The board also noted that top executives like Stumpf and Tolstedt were unwilling to accept criticism when their business model began to fail.[11] It seems a few executives who were unwilling to accept feedback fueled a crushing culture that nearly destroyed the organization's ability to accomplish its mission.

Let's also think about the enormous benefits that come from effective disagreement. The late Steve Jobs, legendary leader of Apple, was famous for his instincts about what consumers wanted. Once his mind was made up, there was little his colleagues could do to change it. Fortunately for us, a few brave souls tried and succeeded.

Initially, Jobs was dead set against making phones. They weren't part of his vision for Apple because a smartphone, by its very nature, was intended for the nerdy, pocket protector crowd, which was the opposite of the elegant, trendy vibe that Jobs sought to create. However, over several years, and with the help of family members, key members of Jobs' team courageously pushed back.

As the story goes, Jobs had a long list of reasons why an Apple phone simply wouldn't work. Tony Fadell, the engineer who created the iPod, and his team spent months working different angles with Jobs. Early on, the team appealed to Jobs' ego by inviting him to consider how beautiful and elegant a phone designed by Apple could be. Later, they played the competition card by asking, what if Mic-

11 Frost, Wilfred. "Wells Fargo report gives inside look at culture that crushed the bank's reputation." CNBC, April 10, 2017. Available at https://www.cnbc.com/2017/04/10/wells-fargo-report-shows-culture-that-crushed-banks-reputation.html (Accessed February 2021).

rosoft creates a phone and we don't? Eventually, the team's mockups and prototypes started to get Jobs' attention, but he was still stuck on how the major carriers had so much control that they could influence the phone's design in ways that made Jobs cringe. Fadell had an answer for that objection, as well: We'll just have to make a phone so good that the carriers will accommodate **us**.

And they did.

Those who have an iPhone know the rest of the story. But there is even further evidence of Jobs' opposition. Even after Jobs finally gave ground on the iPhone, he wasn't about to allow outside apps. Another year of contentious debate convinced him to open the App Store and within nine months, downloads numbered more than one billion. Now, because a few brave people pushed back against strong-willed Jobs' initial decisions, Apple has reaped more than $1 trillion in revenue from the iPhone line, and there's no end in sight.[12]

These examples make the case for healthy opposition, which can only happen when people feel safe in respectfully disagreeing and candidly expressing their objective views about an idea. It stays safe because it doesn't get personal; no one feels at risk. The goal is simply to make the best possible decision, build the best product, or create the most efficient process in support of the mission.

Ideally, opposition evolves into a highly energized form of collaboration.

---

12 Grant, Adam. "Persuading the unpersuadable: Lessons from the science—and the people were able to sway Steve Jobs." *Harvard Business Review*, March-April 2021, pp. 131-135.

> The friction created when different ideas collide
> can serve to sharpen everyone's thinking.

But this won't happen if people aren't willing to speak up or are attacked when they do. When it's safe to objectively disagree and the right people are involved, there is enormous potential for creative solutions, innovation, and new approaches—as well as natural safeguards against really bad ideas, like opening credit card accounts for people who don't want them.

The Components of Healthy Opposition

Healthy opposition requires three components: humility, courage, and respect. If even one is missing, the team will have a tough time finding the benefits of resistance and likely will defer to the person with the highest rank, strongest personality, or loudest voice. And while that person may often have the best ideas, it's unlikely that they will always be right. No one is **always** right. Of course, there's also the option of returning to "the way we've always done it," but that old way of thinking is likely the cause of many of your current problems, especially if the competition has passed you by and innovation is the order of the day.

The positive energy, creativity, and camaraderie present during discussions in which people disagree is impressive. It may seem counterintuitive to think the expression of different views brings people together.

Nevertheless, it works. The paragraphs that follow provide some ideas on how to put the components in place for yourself and others.

Humility. There is something incredibly attractive about a strong, successful person who remains humble. They lower the bar of competition, while increasing opportunities for people to share ideas and accolades. Yet, recognizing their own limitations in no way makes them small or insufficient; rather, they are wise enough to know what they don't know and seek help from those who do.

No leader better exemplifies humility than Mahatma Gandhi, the mild-mannered man who led a nonviolent revolt that ultimately won India's independence from British rule. Some might surmise that Gandhi's posture of humility was forced upon him during the years he had endured racial and religious discrimination, extreme criticism, and even prison; however, his willingness to stand against powerful forces with gentle dignity suggests much more than the response of a broken man. His autobiography reveals an honest self-dissection, noting his propensity to make mistakes, but a willingness to stand corrected and adjust.[13]

Admittedly, Gandhi set an incredibly high, maybe even unattainable standard, for most of us. Instead, we might be more inclined to sing along with Willie Nelson as he belts out:

---

13 Gandhi, M.K. *Gandhi: An Autobiography.* Boston: Beacon Press, 1957.

Oh Lord, it's hard to be humble
When you're perfect in every way
I can't wait to look in the mirror
'Cause I get better looking each day...[14]

It's only natural to smile at these tongue-in-cheek lyrics, but some of us live like the words are sincere. If humility is a challenge, here are some suggestions to foster it:

Recognize that not everything will go your way. Bad stuff happens—sometimes you are the cause; other times, you are collateral damage. After a particularly down week in the markets, Cathie Wood, star money manager and founder of Ark Investment Management, makes this point: "...corrections are good; they keep us all humble."[15]

When things go wrong, **learn.** It's natural to be disappointed when you fall short, but don't beat yourself up and miss the lesson within. When your team misses the mark, conduct an after-action review. The purpose is not to assign blame, but rather to determine how to do better next time.

Embrace feedback. It's easy to accept praise, but critical insights from credible sources hold more value. Access a formal 360-degree assessment, if possible. Otherwise, surround yourself with people

---

14 Davis, Mac (songwriter). "It's Hard to be Humble," Casablanca, 1980.

15 Potter, Sam. "Cathie Wood's funds stabilize after record investor outflows." Bloomberg, February 24, 2021, available at https://www.bloomberg.com/news/articles/2021-02-24/cathie-wood-s-flagship-fund-suffers-biggest-outflow-on-record?s-rnd=premium (Accessed February 2021)

who will tell you the truth, no matter what. Whether it's your spouse, a mentor, or a good friend, give them freedom to tell it like it is. If they hesitate, then they might not be such a good friend after all.

Be grateful. Start by acknowledging the sacrifices and goodwill of others. If you struggle, spend some time examining your family tree to better understand the hardships your ancestors endured so that you could live more comfortably. It's also sobering to consider the millions in this world who live far harder lives than us—and yet the key difference between us and them is opportunity. With practice, you'll find yourself less arrogant and egocentric, and more appreciative of others.

Another great, yet humble leader was Nelson Mandela, who said: "As I have said, the first thing is to be honest with yourself. You can never have an impact on society if you have not changed yourself… Great peacemakers are all people of integrity, of honesty, and humility." [16]

Courage. Healthy opposition to the ideas or actions of others also requires courage. We learn this lesson from a short story by Danish author Hans Christian Andersen that was originally published in 1937. As you may recall, the emperor was so fond of new clothes and looking good that he cared for little else. Eventually, the gullible leader fell prey to a couple of swindlers who promised to create a special outfit out of a fabric that could only be seen by those fit for

---

16 Quotes.net, STANDS4 LLC, 2021. *"Nelson Mandela Quotes."* Accessed February 2021. https://www.quotes.net/quote/49923.

their office and perceptive enough to recognize the great beauty of the magical material.

The crooks demanded a small fortune, then set up looms and pretended to weave. The emperor, anxious for a progress report, sent a trusted old minister to check in on them. Not wanting to reveal his own stupidity, the minister accepted the weavers' description of their exquisite work and gave an excellent report to the emperor. To validate the first man's report, the emperor sent another advisor for a look. By all accounts, the project was going quite well.

Brimming with excitement, the emperor went to see for himself the weavers' beautiful work. Of course, he didn't see anything either, but he, too, kept quiet. When the invisible garments were finally complete, the emperor willingly stripped down to nothing to put on his new clothes.

To great praise from his attendants, the emperor marched pompously out to an awaiting crowd that had gathered to see the grandeur of their leader. Adults immediately praised the emperor's new clothes—despite their inability to see them. Some, not wanting to seem dim, even claimed that they fit to perfection. Finally, a young child quietly announced that the emperor had nothing on.

Eventually, others picked up the child's observation and cried, "But he hasn't got anything on!" Although he feared they might be right, the emperor continued to strut along more proudly than ever, his noble escorts praising his good taste.[17]

---

17 Andersen, Hans Christian. "The Emperor Has No Clothes." Available at https://medium.com/@mattimore/parable-the-emperor-has-no-clothes-ace63fef6eb8. (Accessed

Leaders who surround themselves with agreeable "yes men" often end up making poor decisions with embarrassing results. But, as we chuckle about the emperor's vanity, let's not overlook his associates, who failed him because of their lack of courage. Whether you classify it as moral, professional, or fiduciary responsibility, they should have spoken up when they realized that something wasn't right.

Sadly, this parable plays out in organizations every day. The antidote is having the courage to speak up and the skill to say it in a way that people will hear and understand.

Revisiting the early days of Apple, managers on the Mac team in the 1980s annually recognized an employee who was bold enough to challenge Steve Jobs about something that mattered. Ironically, the winners' courage and skill paid off. Over time, Jobs promoted each one to lead a major department within Apple.[18]

Respect. Ultimately, you provide honest feedback to your peers and direct reports, speak up when something isn't right, and give your best effort because you have respect for yourself and others around you. At this point, you may have respect on autopilot, but there are still reasons for embracing it that are worthy of consideration.

February 2021).

18 Grant, Adam. "Persuading the unpersuadable: Lessons from the science—and the people were able to sway Steve Jobs." *Harvard Business Review*, March-April 2021, pp. 131-135.

Many people of faith embrace the doctrine of Imago Dei, the Latin translation of "image of God." The biblical creation account explains how God created humans in his own image, giving them a special moral, spiritual, and intellectual essence, as well as other unique qualities. Because people are a reflection of God, they deserve dignity, and human life is to be revered. Of course, people have been messing this up since the Garden of Eden, but the standard remains intact.

Because people have long missed the mark on respect, rules have been put in place to guide, protect, and punish. Whether intended to prevent discrimination and harassment, or to open doors for the disabled, these laws are intended to ensure respect in the workplace. Violate the law or your company's rules by disrespecting others and you'll pay a steep price.

Perhaps more relevant are the practical arguments in favor of respect. For example, experience teaches that returns are usually greater when you ask with courtesy and good humor versus barking orders and demanding action. Breaking people down to gain conformance simply doesn't work unless you're a drill sergeant attempting to instill military discipline in a group of raw recruits. Civility is the minimum standard for most organizations, but respect means raising the bar.

To be clear, showing respect to a coworker doesn't mean you like them, would have them babysit your kids, or let them manage your finances. It simply means that you value them as a person and a teammate who can help the team accomplish its mission. Over time, if it turns out that they don't add value or aren't mission essential, they probably shouldn't be on the team. While they're there, though, you have a duty of care toward them.

Duty of care is actually a legal term, but in this context, it suggests that you have some critical obligations if you want your team to be healthy. It's your duty to act in ways that prevent your colleagues from doing things that are harmful to themselves, the team, and the organization. It's your duty to promote fairness, dignity, and professionalism in your interactions. And it's your duty to keep an open mind, actively listen, and give people a voice. Everyone, no matter their role or rank, has the duty of care.

Safety First, Safety Always

Everyone should demonstrate respect, but leaders have the unique duty to create safe opportunities for people to disagree. However, I fear there may be confusion as to how it's done, based on responses I received to real-time survey questions asked in hundreds of classrooms and meeting rooms over the years.

When discussing the importance of healthy opposition with students, I'll often pause to ask: "By show of hands, how many of you believe it's okay, or safe, for your team members to respectfully disagree with you?" Inevitably, nearly every hand in the room goes up. Encouraged, I then ask: "Can you say the same for **every** manager in your organization, including **your** manager?" Sadly, rarely is a single hand raised. Instead, people lower their eyes and shake their heads. That suggests something is wrong.

The problem likely boils down to a disconnect between how people believe they are perceived and what those around them actually think. As to whether people feel safe to disagree, the difference is enormous; however, you can bridge the gap with a rock solid commitment to open-door and open-eared leadership.

The term "psychological safety" was coined by Harvard Business School professor Amy Edmondson, and its definition is clear: "Psychological safety is a belief that one will not be punished or humiliated for speaking up with ideas, questions, concerns, or mistakes."[19] It matters because teammates learn better, perform better, and feel better about each other and their work when they feel safe.

Seems like common sense, right? But if you're a data-driven person, then consider the findings of Project Aristotle, the famous Google study of factors that most influence team effectiveness. Over a two-year span, some of the best and brightest people analysts studied 180 Google teams, conducted more than 200 in-depth interviews, and analyzed some 250 attributes of success, yet they struggled to pin down the most important ingredient for team success. Then, they began to sharpen their focus on group norms, or the intangible rules that govern how people interact.

---

19 Amy Edmondson. 1999. "Psychological Safety and Learning Behavior in Work Teams." *Administrative Science Quarterly* 44 (2): 350–83. https://doi.org/10.2307/2666999.

Many of the characteristics associated with the norms of high-performing teams have been covered in previous chapters: clarity of mission, making the mission meaningful to the people involved, and commitment. But the factor that profoundly outdistanced the others in this study was psychological safety. And the teams that excelled were the ones where people felt free to be themselves without every word and action being subject to harsh criticism.[20]

The findings of Project Aristotle were more precise on one interesting point, though. Members of the highest-performing teams all talked roughly the same amount of time. No individual dominated every conversation. Obviously, the manager—and/or the person who tended to dominate—kept quiet at times so that others could speak.

The finding also suggests that the people on these teams felt included and that their contributions truly made a difference. It's one thing to hire a diverse team, but it's a far different thing to give each person a voice. It's possible that people find their voice when they know there won't be repercussions for saying something inconsistent with precedent or even a little crazy at the time. On these high-performing teams, the research found that mistakes were considered opportunities for learning and growth.

While all of this sounds great in general, here are some specific suggestions that every leader can employ to increase psychological safety:

---

20   Schneider, Michael. "Google spent 2 years studying 180 teams. The most successful ones shared these 5 traits." *Inc*, July 19, 2017, available at https://www.inc.com/ michael-schneider/google-thought-they-knew-how-to-create-the-perfect.html (Accessed February 2021).

Model vulnerability. We have already established that you're not perfect, so why pretend to be? In this regard, the idiom "warts and all" and the legend of its origin come to mind. According to the story that didn't emerge until long after his death, Oliver Cromwell, during his time as Lord Protector of the Commonwealth, invited Sir Peter Lely to paint his portrait. Instead of asking the famous artist to portray him as a dashing and cavalier military strategist turned statesman, Cromwell instructed Lely to paint him as he really appeared—warts and all. If the story is true, it would seem that Cromwell favored authenticity as a way to align himself with more common people rather than the Royalists he had long fought against.[21]

There is something appealing about leaders who are secure enough to not hide behind the pretense of having all the answers or being in control. When they do take control, team members generally remain talkative, as far as sharing ideas or speaking up when they disagree. As in all cases, good boundaries are in order for the sake of decorum, plus one's warts don't morph into a license to be an insufferable bore. However, allowing a few warts to show at times can let others know you need their help.

Actively listen. Asking people to speak up requires you to listen— even if you don't like it. I've noticed that certain people have a gift for being fully present and focused on whoever is speaking to them. Even in a crowded room that is bustling with activity, the gifted

---

21 Castelow, Ellen. "Oliver Cromwell." *Historic UK*, available at https://www.historic-uk.com/HistoryUK/HistoryofEngland/Oliver-Cromwell/ (Accessed February 2021).

listener is completely engaged and acts as if no one else is around. To see one of these people in action is to be amazed at how others react to them.

Several years ago, I had the opportunity to present a series of events with author and psychologist Dr. Henry Cloud. During breaks or after speaking, Henry was always very gracious about interacting with attendees, and I often found myself standing a few feet away—not to eavesdrop, but to watch. As long lines of people formed to chat with him or get a book signed, he would lean in, lock eyes with them, and sincerely ask a question that would start the conversation. He never seemed hurried, distracted, or less than fascinated by each word said. Often, I'd have to politely interrupt one of these conversations so we could resume the session.

Henry never failed to impress both me and those who attended his presentations. Many expressed how meaningful it was to have a brief one-on-one conversation with Henry. And though I don't know what was actually said in any of those conversations, my observations suggest that Henry never spoke more than 20% of the time. He was simply a great listener.

Share the air. I had never really thought about it before I began researching for this book, but it rings true to Google's Project Aristotle study that the best—those that did incredible work and had fun doing it—were like a band of brothers (and sisters). We all had something to say and we didn't hesitate to say it. The teams I couldn't wait to leave had one or two people that dominated every conversation.

Of course, there will always be the outgoing and vocal extroverts, while others are introverts and tend to hold back. Neither is better; people are just different. But with this in mind, it's important to invite the quieter people to share their thoughts, perhaps giving them some advance notice instead of putting them on the spot. Encourage them with a prompt that speaks to their expertise or experience in a particular area. And if a more vocal colleague attempts to cut them off, step in. After a few prompts like, "Wait, let's allow Jill to finish her thought," other team members will get the message that everyone's input is, in fact, valuable.

Don't hammer people. If you've been in the working world more than a few days, this idiom likely makes sense. If, however, you've spent your entire life in a perpetual place of happiness and sunshine, where everyone is always kind and loving, and you got a trophy for showing up, then let me be more precise. It means that you can't expect people to speak up if there is a valid reason for them to believe they will be criticized, made to feel stupid, embarrassed, punished for a mistake, given extra work, put on the hot seat with 54 additional questions, or made an example of. Now, do you get it?

Conclusion

Over the last few years, I have informally polled about 5,000 people with experience working on teams. I begin by asking whether anyone in the room has been on a team where there was no healthy opposition—one of those go-along-and-get-along operations where (1) no one wants to rock the boat, and (2) people learn quickly that opposing the manager's idea can lead to trouble that nobody wants. Inevitably, a significant portion of every group raises their hands in agreement.

My next question is: "How many of you would give that team's output (performance) the letter grade of A?" Rarely does a single hand go up. As I go down the grade scale, I see more hands when I get to C and C-minus, but most go up when I call out D and F grades. With the visual evidence in place, I again make the point that healthy opposition—as long as it is objective and professional—helps teams perform better. Those teams also are likely to accomplish their mission.

exercise

This leaves a few important questions for you:
- What grade has your team earned for its performance of late?
- Are you satisfied or can you do better?
- How do you move up to or maintain an A or A+ grade for your team's performance?

Based on your answers, a little more opposition might be in order. Continue thinking about where your team is now and where you want to take them as you answer the following reflection questions.

reflection

Spend as much time as needed to answer the following questions about whether you and your team are embracing healthy opposition. Try to think of specific examples that support your answers, as they will serve as evidence that you are on the right path or show that you need to make adjustments.

- Do you often find yourself in "the meeting after the meeting?" Are you more comfortable addressing certain issues with a close-knit group of confidants than with the broader team and more senior executives who might benefit from hearing your point of view? If so, why?

- Does your team regularly have healthy opposition? How would you describe those conversations? What are the benefits and risks?

- How often do you concede a point or feign agreement just to move on? What are the consequences for you, your team, and the project?

- How does your team display humility, courage, and respect? What have you done to make those qualities cultural norms for your team or organization?
- Who on your team is most likely to speak up and engage in debate about the merits of different approaches? How do you feel about them? Do you respect them more or less than the agreeable people who seem to always go with the flow?
- What have you done in the last month to create a comfortable environment for your teammates to engage in healthy opposition?
- On your team, does everyone speak about the same amount of time?

action items

After reflecting on the preceding questions, choose one or more of the action items below to place on your to-do list this week or month. Over time, work through the list. If you are consistent and make habits of these actions, you will likely see a good return on your investment.

- When you have an opposing view regarding a policy or process, courageously speak up. Use a candid, professional, and respectful approach to make your ideas known to key stakeholders, while understanding that your idea may not be best or the one that is accepted.

· Managers should encourage their teams to discuss and debate different approaches and provide time for it in meetings. Explain why healthy opposition is so important and that you are committed to making it safe for people to disagree.

· At your next meeting, ask for input from those who often stay quiet. These people often have the best ideas. Consider alerting them before the meeting that you will be asking for their input so they can prepare.

· Call a team meeting or off-site gathering and create a team charter focused on how your team will handle opposing views. Endorse specific examples of humility, courage, and respect, and gain the team's commitment to practice these and similar behaviors to promote healthy opposition.

additional reading

Think Again: The Power of Knowing What You Don't Know, Adam Grant, Viking, 2021.

Difficult Conversations: How to Discuss What Matters Most, Douglas Stone, Bruce Patton, and Sheila Heen, Penguin, 2010.

the conflict chronicles

how to change the story

A FEW YEARS AGO, I was invited to work with a midsized financial services firm in the Midwest. Apparently, my book— *Have a Nice Conflict: How to Find Success and Satisfaction in the Most Unlikely Places*—had caught the attention of the human resources director. His initial phone message went something like this: "We have a new chief operating officer. Her name is Mary…and when things go wrong around here, she is hell on wheels! She rants and raves, and honestly, she's scaring more than a few people. It's just not good! Can you help?"

Being the good consultant that I am, I returned his call and arranged a visit. I arrived to find that the HR leader had gathered all of the executives in a conference room. They were pleasant enough and fairly diverse, but because of the part of the country we were in, there were more than a few good ol' boys whose business casual attire included cowboy boots and, in some cases, saucer-sized belt buckles.

As I made the rounds greeting everyone, I came to a petite, middle-aged woman with thick, snow-white hair. She looked a bit like former first lady Barbara Bush, who I always respected, so that gave her immediate credibility in my mind. Smiling broadly, she stuck out her hand and brightly proclaimed, "I'm Mary, the chief operating officer."

Instantly, I blurted out: "So you're Scary Mary! How can it be?"

As the designated expert on conflict management, I didn't want to be duped by her pleasant demeanor and small stature. Could this all be a well-honed act that cleverly disguised the monster who had been wreaking havoc with the staff? I had to stay alert.

Of course, Mary didn't know quite what to make of my outburst, but she let it slide and we began the meeting. As we talked about conflict, we eventually dug into what made Mary so scary to the rest of the group. Fortunately, where we started and where we ended were very different places. In reality, Mary was a very nice person. She was open and sincerely wanted to share her perspective with the rest of the team. She was also a good listener and wanted to hear from others to understand how she had made them feel. One unexpected thing we discovered was that, when Mary initially experienced conflict, she was not especially angry.

At first, this was difficult for her colleagues to accept. After all, she often raised her voice, became direct, and was quite forceful. At one point, Mary acknowledged that when she behaved in that way, it evoked responses in people that she didn't necessarily want. She even said she was aware that some of the cowboys in the crowd—who probably outweighed her by well over 125 pounds—were left cowering in the men's room waiting for the storm to pass. While some of the men mumbled their disagreement about Mary's use of the word "cowering," they did acknowledge that they occasionally needed some time to think—in private—about what had gone wrong and how best to respond.

Mary was on a roll, and so was the conversation. She corrected teammates who were quick to apologize and placate. Surprisingly, she invited everyone in the group to bring their ideas and push back if they believed their way was better.

Mary finally paused for a breath, so I jumped in to ask what it was she really wanted in times of conflict. As she paused to think, I revisited Elias Porter's definition of conflict[1] I had written on the whiteboard earlier:

> "Conflict is an emotional response to a perceived threat to my values or sense of self-worth,"

---

and I reminded everyone that how each of us responds to conflict is our way of defending what's important.

Finally, Mary responded. Her few, carefully chosen words—"I want to fix it fast"—were like turning the lights on in a pitch-black room, and they were my opening to further illuminate. Because Mary valued progress and momentum toward company goals, she sometimes experienced conflict when she saw stuff not getting done. As a result, Mary focused all of her energy on "fixing it fast" to get the team back on track toward mission accomplishment.

---

1 Porter, Elias H. "On the Development of Relationship Awareness Theory: A Personal Note." Group & Organization Management 1, no. 3 (1976): 302-09.

"Look," she said. "I get that I can come on pretty strong at times, but it's because I care so much about serving our customers. We have responsibilities to them, so I immediately want to address anything that gets in our way. And I need all of you to help me do it."

Immediately, I could see others in the room start to relax. After all, Mary's intentions were certainly good. The team began to relax even more upon realizing she wasn't an angry person ready to fire people at the drop of a hat. Soon, however, a contemplative cowboy from the back of the room voiced the question that was still at the top of everyone's mind: "Why is it so hard to get things done when there is conflict?

It's Complicated. Conflict keeps us from doing our best work because we move to defend our values instead of driving toward what's important. To borrow a sports metaphor, conflict can cause us to take our eye off the ball. Additionally, its causes and how we respond varies based on each person's unique personality.

This is why I prefer the SDI 2.0's view of personality. The assessment results show how conflict can be triggered, and how people are likely to respond with a predictable Conflict Sequence[2]. In other words, my reaction when I perceive that I'm under attack will very likely be different than yours—and the trigger might differ, as well.

The Marys of the world want to assert themselves, address every issue head-on, and fix it fast. Other people want to accommodate

---

2 Scudder, Tim. *Working with SDI 2.0*. Carlsbad, CA: Core Strengths, 2021. Note: The term "Conflict Sequence" and the descriptive words, "accommodate, assert, and analyze" used in this section are from this book.

and are likely to make apologies or concessions in order to maintain peace and harmony. Still others want to analyze, slow things down, pull back, and think it through before acting. They replay conversations in their head repeatedly, trying to figure out how in the world they ever got into this mess. That takes time, so when Mary starts pushing them to get moving, they may not be ready. Of course, this further frustrates Mary, she pushes harder, others become even more stuck in analysis mode, and mission progress slows to a crawl.

People will try different approaches when it becomes clear that their initial attempt at resolving conflict isn't working. They shift their defensive posture and become more self-focused, making these situations even more confusing and difficult to navigate. This, as we explained earlier, was why some people found Mary's assertive behavior to be over the top and even threatening.

Mary's strong and more direct reaction represented how they would act when they were much deeper into the conflict, had already tried other ways to resolve it, and now were ready to take people out. In other words, they see Mary's more energized, confrontational approach as something they would do at the end of the line, not the outset. They often believe Mary is blowing things out of proportion and see her behavior as, well, a bit scary. Mary maintains that she is simply making a rapid course correction, so the team doesn't stray too far off track. The different approaches to dealing with conflict, and the different filters through which others see them, help us understand why interpersonal conflict can be so tricky to navigate.

Our interpretation of someone's behavior can miss the mark in terms of what is driving that behavior. Psychologists call this the false-consensus effect, or consensus bias.[3] It's one of the most pervasive forms of cognitive bias and is a tough one to overcome. If you don't guard against it, however, you risk believing that there is something wrong with those who dare to disagree with you. These biased beliefs affect workplace relationships and your performance.

Conflict is Costly. We've established that opposition is good. Now, let's look at how bickering is bad. Interpersonal conflict comes at a high price and makes it tough—but not impossible—to accomplish the mission.

There are a number of ways to calculate the cost of conflict in organizations. Let's look at a few:

Conflict causes us to waste time. Consider all of the hours people spend bickering or brooding, or gossiping about the bickering and brooding of others. Researchers have determined that, on average, U.S. workers spend almost three hours per week dealing with conflict. By applying an average hourly wage and doing the math, it comes up to $359 billion in lost productivity each year. Sadly, according to the same study, 29% of employees experience conflict almost constantly.[4]

---

3 Ross Lee, David Greene, and Pamela House. 1977. "The 'False Consensus Effect': An Egocentric Bias in Social Perception and Attribution Processes." *Journal of Experimental Social Psychology* 13 (3): 279–301. https://doi.org/10.1016/0022-1031(77)90049-X.

4 CPP. Human Capital Report, 2008, available at https://www.themyersbriggs.com (Accessed March 2021).

Conflict sometimes brings legal costs. Interpersonal conflict causes us to treat people badly, make people feel that they are being treated badly, or more likely, a bit of both. Unfortunately, this keeps HR and legal professionals busy. In 2019, the Equal Employment Opportunity Commission (EEOC) received 72,675 claims of discrimination, which led to about $50 million in damages paid to victims by their employers.[5] Apart from the EEOC, about 12% of employers are hit with an employment lawsuit each year; each suit, on average, costs about $125,000 to defend. When a case goes to court, the median judgment for plaintiffs is $200,000, plus substantial legal costs.[6]

Conflict causes turnover. In survey after survey, one of the top reasons people give for leaving a job is a poor relationship (i.e., conflict) with their manager.[7] Other research from Columbia University suggests that turnover triples when an organization's culture is deemed poor by employees.[8] And we all know how tough it is to find the right replacement.

---

5 U.S. Equal Employment Opportunity Commission, 2020, available at https://www.eeoc.gov/statistics/charge-statistics-charges-filed-eeoc-fy-1997-through-fy-2020 (Accessed March 2021).

6 Hiscox, 2015 Hiscox Guide to Employee Lawsuits, available at https://www.hiscox.com/newsroom/press/hiscox-study-reveals-states-with-highest-employee-lawsuit-risk (Accessed March 2021).

7 "Why people quit their jobs," *Harvard Business Review*, September 2016, available at https://hbr.org/2016/09/why-people-quit-their-jobs#:~:text=In%20general%2C%20people%20leave%20their,have%20held%20steady%20for%20years. (Accessed March 2021).

8 Graham, John, Grennan, Jillian, Campbell, Harvey, and Rajgopal, Shivaram, 2018. "Corporate culture: Evidence from the field." Columbia Business School Research Paper No. 16-49.

Conflict causes absenteeism and presenteeism. As many continue to work from home because of COVID-19, absenteeism in the traditional sense—people not showing up for work—may not be as evident. But where an employee's physical presence is mission critical, absenteeism remains a major concern. Again, research tells us that up to 25% of absenteeism is attributable to people not wanting to deal with an interpersonal conflict at work.[9] Presenteeism is a less-used term, but it describes people who are there, collecting a paycheck, but not contributing much. In some cases, they poison the culture and inhibit progress. Regardless of age, we sometimes refer to these straphangers as "retired on duty."

Conflict causes stress, sleep loss, and health issues. Who hasn't lost sleep because of conflict with a colleague or manager, or the anticipation of what might happen in tomorrow's meeting? I had a bright, young sales professional tell me once that she became physically ill—to the point of throwing up—before each scheduled meeting with her manager. A senior manager in a federal law enforcement agency shared that he developed an ulcer and saw his marriage relationship decline over the 18 months or so he had reported to a particular commanding officer. Fortunately, within six months of his retirement, the ulcer was gone and his marriage was strong again.

Of course, there are myriad other costs associated with conflict, but you get the idea. In our context, the greatest concern is how interpersonal conflict can impede mission progress. That alone is

9 CPP. Human Capital Report, 2008, available at https://www.themyersbriggs.com (Accessed March 2021).

enough to make our top priority understanding how to prevent and manage conflict, but mitigating some of the costs creates even more reason to stay focused.

Prevent Conflict with a Proactive Approach.

The best conflict strategy is to prevent it from happening at all.

Notice that I didn't use "avoid" because it has a different meaning. Perhaps a metaphor will help.

If there is a big pothole in a busy street, you'll do your best to avoid hitting it because the jolt could do real damage to your car and might cause you to spill your coffee. On days when you're thinking about your next meeting or some urgent errand, you may hit the pothole hard and feel the teeth-rattling reminder that it's still there. On other days, weather conditions or traffic may keep you from swerving to miss the hole, and now you need yet another front-end alignment that costs time and money. The obvious problem with this avoidance strategy is that it doesn't always work.

Prevention, on the other hand, involves taking the initiative to maintain the streets to keep everyone moving smoothly toward their destination.

Conflict isn't much different. A previous rocky experience may cause you to avoid someone, perhaps using elaborate work-around or fly-under-the-radar strategies to evade detection. When there's a confrontation, the avoidance strategy can send you careening into a ditch with visions of missed deadlines and unhappy stakeholders. Again, conflict avoidance is neither foolproof nor sustainable.

A more proactive prevention strategy is to truly learn what triggers conflict for you and others—ideally, by using a valid and reliable assessment like the SDI 2.0—and then, with resolve, to honor the values of everyone involved. For example, if I know that a colleague values being well prepared for meetings—because she hates being caught by surprise—then the wise and respectful thing to do is to provide her with a detailed agenda before the meeting. If the boss values brevity, I shouldn't go in with a long, rambling story that leaves her waiting for the punch line. Returning to the pothole metaphor, it's making sure there is no hole to fall into because I have cultivated a strong relationship with my coworker.

This prevention concept is not terribly difficult. In most cases, it simply requires a little forethought, attention to the needs of others, and perhaps a dash of flexibility. A little interpersonal agility will help prevent a time-consuming relational collision. The only requirement is to know your colleagues well enough to know their work styles and communication preferences, and then you must remain nimble enough to make the proper adjustments.

Alan Gilbert, the famous former music director of the New York Philharmonic orchestra, recognized that he could get much more out of his musicians by getting to know them rather than viewing them in the traditional, subservient role under the maestro's baton.[10] And because their collective mission is to deliver moving and memorable musical performances, Gilbert recognized that it was worth the effort.

Don't React—Respond. None of us can prevent every conflict. When you find yourself shifting into defensive mode—or, worse yet, facing a Scary Mary—don't react. Instead, respond. Your natural reaction to conflict is designed to serve and protect you. Others may need something else from you in that moment, which may not help with the mission. So, your natural reaction to conflict may temporarily interrupt your mission focus.

A better approach to conflict management is to thoughtfully choose how you're going to respond, keeping in mind that this choice will affect both relationships and results. Consider the following six important questions. Because conflict is emotional and sometimes heated, working through these questions will allow you to slow down, reboot your brain, and behave rationally, even as your emotions want to pull you into fight, flight, or freeze mode.

What good intentions are driving that person's behavior? Unless you work with sociopaths, which you probably don't unless you toil in a particularly harsh prison or a locked-down mental health facility, most of your coworkers are trying to do what they believe is good and right. If you can stay focused on that point, you may be able to avoid some time-consuming conflicts.

---

10 Lawson, Wayne. "Exit interview: Maestro Alan Gilbert prepares for life after Lincoln Center." *Vanity Fair*, June 8, 2017, available at https://www.vanityfair.com/style/2017/06/alan-gilbert-new-york-philharmonic-exit-interview (Accessed March 2021).

By simply opening your mind to why a person said or did something you saw as unwise, you can slow your emotions and avoid jumping to conclusions. Besides, who wants to be consumed with suspicion, mistrust, and dark calculations?

Of course, this is not to suggest that you be naïve or let people take advantage. There are plenty of folks out there who will readily hurt others to get their way. There are also many in corporate environments who play politics and run power plays to get ahead. Nevertheless, you have to engage people to accomplish the mission. Working to recognize their productive motives helps.

Are they really attacking me? One of the first and most important choices you must make is whether you are truly under attack or perhaps are being a little too sensitive. You'll also need to determine whether the alleged slight is important enough to knock you off your game—even for a moment—or if the person who hurled it your way is a credible source and worth your precious time. In short, will you let yourself be sucked in? The great news is that your answer can always be no.

Although tiny, "no" is the most empowering word in the English (or Spanish) language. It puts you in the driver's seat and seizes control from the person or situation that is trying to run you into an emotional ditch. You make this decision easier by reflecting on whether the other person's snide remark is even about you or is driven by something going on within themselves. Did something unpleasant happen at home this morning? Are they struggling with life issues that you may not fully understand? You may not know the answers, but simply asking the questions prevents you from you ceding control of your emotions to someone else.

Any disagreement that isn't personal has the potential to improve performance. Also, always remember that you control your emotions, and you decide whether you're going to treat the situation as healthy opposition or a potentially devastating conflict.

What matters most in this moment? Of course, the mission should always be a top consideration. However, you must also balance other important concerns that clearly fall into the "people always" column. The theme of this book is that performance and people are always linked. Since one can't exist without the other, you have to strike a balance.

This high-wire balancing act was never clearer than during the early days of the COVID-19 pandemic in 2020. Many companies had to make gut-wrenching decisions to let good employees go because otherwise, the enterprise would not survive. Executives—and especially small-business owners—were desperately trying to survive. Some reasoned that without the mission, people would have no place to which they could return when the world reopened.

Other times, what matters most in the moment is less clear. An experienced manager who successfully navigated a tricky situation in the past could up the odds of success in the present by simply telling her people what to do and how to do it, even though some team members might not appreciate the heavy-handed approach. However, she might choose a less-directive way to let the team work through the process and become more resourceful.

Families often find themselves in these murky waters. When spouses want different things, there will be conflict unless they can find a compromise. Whether it's a simple decision, like going to the beach or the mountains for vacation, those involved have to decide what matters most: getting their way or responding in a way that strengthens the relationship. With kids, it's often a choice between protecting them or allowing them to learn on their own. Should you help with their science project so they get an "A" that puts them on the fast track to the Ivy League or let them flounder and learn the resilience they'll need to get through State U? These are all tough calls, but it is imperative to ask what matters most before deciding your direction.

What can I do right now that moves me toward what really matters? Once you've decided what matters most, get moving. If the risk factor is high without you taking charge, jump in. If the first priority is for others to learn and grow, delegate authority to show trust in your team. The key is being intentional so that your actions support a thoughtful decision. Some people allow their emotions to guide them, which is never a good way to operate.

It's almost always good to explain to people who matter both your actions and the motives behind them. Otherwise, they may draw their own (wrong) conclusions. Such transparency breeds trust and demonstrates that you're acting with integrity—your heart, words, and actions are aligned (integrated). Few things are worse than a disingenuous leader who says one thing and does another.

What matters to them? Managing conflict is a two-way street that requires considering the values of others. The mere presence of conflict means that somehow, someone got the impression that something important to them was under attack—by you, someone else, or maybe even forces that can't be pinned on a particular person. Determining what caused the conflict provides key insight on what's important to them. This information can also help you target your response and point your team member back to a more productive place.

At this point, it might seem that you need the other-worldly powers of a clairvoyant or Sherlock Holmes-level observational skills to make any of this work. Truth is, you can gain much insight by listening to what people say, watching what they do, and asking good questions to fill in the blanks.

As practice, think about what matters so much that if those values were violated, it might trigger conflict in you. I often ask this and similar questions in workshops and am always fascinated by the answers.

Recently, I asked a group of production managers from a large consumer products company what really ticks them off at work. One manager said it drives him crazy when a colleague wants to act based on an irrational, half-baked idea that has trickle-down effects that were never considered. He asked, "Why can't people take the time to do their homework, and think things through before recommending—or worse yet, taking—action?"

Clearly, this manager values a thoughtful process that takes into account all of the ramifications of a decision; therefore, if these values are violated, you would probably need to go back and methodically work with him through the process and implications of the decision to address his concerns.

Another manager piped in to say that her hot button was negativity—i.e., the Debbie Downers who fabricate multiple reasons that something can't be done before the idea is fully presented. "I hate negativity," she said.

Aggressive nitpicking by colleagues can violate this value, so you might see her go into conflict. Recognizing this puts you in good position to constructively respond. It could be as simple as expressing your appreciation for her optimism and can-do spirit, and then focusing on how to make her idea even better so that her vision can be fulfilled in the face of real-world constraints. By the way, you're not suggesting that her colleagues' concerns are invalid; rather, you're demonstrating respect for their enthusiasm and desire to do big things. From that perspective, she might be ready to re-engage in a more productive discussion about how to make her idea work.

Yet another workshop group was itching to respond. (If the setting is right, people find it quite easy to talk about what ticks them off.) In near unison, they said it really bothers them when team members lack the agility to pivot in response to new information.

They resented closed-minded people who felt their way was the only right way to do something.

The answers to this simple question of what matters to folks yielded tremendous insight for managing conflict. By the way, I didn't know any of these people before the workshop, so I didn't have any relational experience to draw upon. I had not seen how they react to stressful situations, interacted with them in meetings, nor had I worked on projects with them. I simply asked a question and listened. Anyone can do that and so much more when it comes to knowing what matters most to your colleagues.

How can I build a bridge? The imagery of conflict often includes battle lines with an expanse between two opposing forces. The distance provides some sense of security for the combatants while they prepare for the next skirmish, but it also creates a no-man's land where no one is really safe. It's no place to be unless you are particularly courageous and are attempting to end the hostilities.

This same symbolism applies to interpersonal conflict because it divides the people involved. They may occupy the same physical space, but there are emotional gaps that cripple their ability to work in harmony.

This sense of separation often keeps people from talking to each other and, more importantly, listening to what each other has to say. It impinges upon collaboration because sharing one's ideas and inviting constructive critiques require people to be open and vulnerable. By definition, conflict puts people into a defensive posture that limits their willingness to be exposed.

This gap must be bridged by meeting others where they are and giving them what they need.

Despite my earlier symbolism, enemy lines must never exist on a mission first, people always team. Instead, bridges should provide pathways for reconnection.

For those who tend to be a bit skeptical, know that my suggestion to build bridges and give people what they need does not indicate that you are wrong, they are right, and you need to make amends. Instead, the bridge where you can meet people where they are and give them what they need is intended to move you from debilitating conflict to healthy opposition. Then, you can discuss and debate ideas, perhaps concluding that your idea is, in fact, best—but you're doing it in a way that allows everyone to stay productively engaged.

When Scary Mary was energized around fixing a problem fast, teammates were inclined to retreat or concede. This isn't what Mary wanted or needed in that moment. Instead, she wanted people to step up, share her conviction about the mission (fixing the problem fast), and get busy. At one point in our conversation, Mary even said she would welcome alternative solutions. In other words, if your idea is better, bring it and let the best idea win, as long as it serves the mission.

Mary also recognized during our discussion that she might get better results if she met people where they are in conflict. For her cowboy hat-wearing colleagues, Mary could press the pause button to give them a little time and space to formulate their thoughts. I suggested that even an hour or two would help and then, together, they could resolve the issue by end of day. And to those who immediately start making concessions when they sense something is wrong, Mary might emphasize that she is not angry at them—or anyone else, for that matter—rather, she is just focused on how to best serve customers. That might calm their fears and get them involved in finding the right solution.

At the end of the day with Mary's team, we were in a much better place. With the new insight everyone now shared, "scary" no longer accurately described Mary. Instead, she was seen as someone who colleagues viewed as highly committed to the mission in good times and bad, and who was equally devoted to bringing out the best in her team when the road became rocky. This new fear-free culture also meant less time cowering and more time collaborating. All in all, it was a good day.

reflection

Spend as much time as needed to answer the following questions about how conflict is affecting your performance. Specific examples will provide deeper insight and help to guide the adjustments you need to make.

- How has interpersonal conflict interfered with your team's performance in the last few months?
- What triggers conflict for you at work? How do these things relate to what matters most to you?
- What are you taking a little too personal that could be chalked up to a difference of opinion?
- Are there people on your team you need to see through the lens of positive intent? What would happen if you did?
- What triggers conflict for your manager, key colleagues, direct reports, and spouse? Tip: The answer isn't the same for all of these people.
- Do you avoid certain people for fear that your interaction with them might be unpleasant or even lead to conflict? How well has your avoidance strategy worked?
- Do you have a Scary Mary in your world? When this person comes at you in conflict, what are your first thoughts and reactions?

action items

After reflecting on the questions above, choose one or more of the action items below to place on your to-do list this week or this month. Over time, work through the list. If you are consistent and make habits of these actions, you will likely see a good return on your investment.

- Complete the Calculating the Cost of Conflict Worksheet in the appendix. Discuss the results with your manager.
- Identify the conflict triggers for each person on your team.
- Let your direct reports know what irritates you at work. That way, they will know what not to do.
- Create a conflict charter for your team. This is a series of agreements and commitments you make to each other about how you will handle interpersonal conflict.
- The next time you find yourself in conflict with a coworker, make an effort to meet them where they are to give them what they need. Feel free to try this approach with your spouse or a friend. The benefits that come from applying this skill are often far greater at home than at work.

additional reading

Have a Nice Conflict: How to Find Success and Satisfaction in the Most Unlikely Places, Tim Scudder, Michael Patterson & Kent Mitchell, Jossey-Bass, 2012.

people are always watching

what do they see?

THE HEADLINE MADE me uncomfortable: "Hackers Breach Thousands of Security Cameras, Exposing Tesla, Jails, Hospitals."[1]

The news report described how hackers had broken through the cyber-security defenses of Verkada Inc., a Silicon Valley startup. The intrusion opened access to the live feeds of 150,000 surveillance cameras inside companies like Tesla and software provider Cloudfare Inc., as well as prisons, police departments, women's health clinics, and schools.

Some of the hacked systems used facial-recognition technology to identify the people on camera, so any thoughts of anonymity were dashed, as well. One of the more disturbing scenes showed what appeared to be eight hospital staffers in Florida tackling a patient and pinning him to a bed. Ironically, that particular hospital had just been featured in a news report about how its recently installed security system complied with all medical privacy laws.

---

1 Turton, William, March 10, 2021. "Hackers breach thousands of security cameras, exposing Tesla, jails, hospitals." Bloomberg, available at https://www.bloombergquint. com/business/hackers-expose-tesla-jails-in-breach-of-150-000-security-cams (Accessed March 2021).

Now, I'm not the guy who puts a sticky note or piece of tape over my computer monitor's camera, but this article gave me pause about how much of everyday life is not as private as we may think. My investigation also revealed that China has deployed 200 million closed-circuit TV cameras in its sovereign territory to monitor the population. Then, just as I was getting worked up over government intrusion by totalitarian regimes, I discovered that the United States has 50 million devices installed—the most per capita in the world. London and New Delhi made the world's top-10 list for cities with the most closed-circuit cameras.[2]

Many argue that the cameras are there to protect us from terrorists, criminals, and other miscreants who seek to harm us. Indeed, there was more privacy and far fewer security cameras prior to 9/11; however, thankfully, the events we now capture on camara leads to action that makes us safer.

Dr. Martin Luther King, Jr. recognized the importance of using visual evidence, often in the form of brutal and disturbing images, to spark change. After one of many peaceful protests in which marchers were roughed up by police, King reportedly scolded *Life* magazine photographer Flip Schulke for helping protestors who had been

---

2 MTS Staff Writer, December 5, 2019, "USA has highest number of CCTV cameras per person in the world." Mertechseries, available at https://martechseries.com/technology/usa-highest-number-cctv-cameras-per-person-world/#:~:text=They%20have%20established%20over%20200,and%20control%20its%20civil%20population.&text=China%20is%20followed%20by%20the,place%20with%205%20million%20cameras. (Accessed March 2021).

knocked down instead of continuing to snap photos.[3] Without the photos, King said, the world would not know what was happening and nothing would change.

Fortunately, TV cameras captured deputies on horseback and Alabama state troopers brutally attacking John Lewis and the 600 marchers trying to make their way across the Edmund Pettus Bridge in Selma, AL. The undeniable images, seen amidst clouds of tear gas, so greatly shocked the conscious of the nation that Bloody Sunday became a turning point in the American civil-rights movement.

A little more than 25 years later, appalling footage captured by a bystander with a camcorder led to something far different than peaceful protests. Perhaps it's because I lived and worked in Los Angeles at the time that I so distinctly remember the first time I saw the footage of LAPD officers repeatedly striking Rodney King with their batons. A little more than a year later, live news chopper coverage showed Reginald Denny being pulled from his truck at Florence and Normandie avenues in South Los Angeles, where he was nearly beaten to death by an angry mob.

Within a few hours of the Denny incident, my California Army National Guard unit was activated, and I found myself leading heavily armed soldiers in defense of the city. Burning buildings, faces of angry protestors, and the eerie presence of many military vehicles on the streets of a major American city are images that I

---

3 Roberts, Gene, and Hank Klibanoff. 2006. *The Race Beat: The Press, the Civil Rights Struggle, and the Awakening of a Nation.* 1st ed. New York: Knopf.

simply can't unsee. Sadly, we continue to see images of scenes we wish did not happen.

With smartphone cameras and social media, now everyone can capture and broadcast events as they occur. Oftentimes, these scenes make us shudder, but just as Dr. King recognized, the ability to see violent abuses of power is an impetus for much-needed reform. Unfortunately, change doesn't come without great cost. The names of victims like George Floyd, Rayshard Brooks, Daniel Prude, Philando Castile, and many others are widely known only because we saw what happened to them.

These dark images and the names associated with them are burned into our memories because what we saw moved us. Fortunately, we are also affected by the good and beautiful things we see. Whether it be medical workers covered head to toe with personal protective equipment, feverishly working to save someone's life; a firefighter carrying a child out of a burning building; or an elderly veteran saluting the flag at a Memorial Day ceremony—these images move us, too. Hopefully, we are consumed by gratitude, pride, or resolve to become a better version of ourselves because of what we see.

Like it or not, people are always watching. But for leaders trying to strike the balance between people and performance, the real question is, what are they seeing? The simple and perhaps frustrating answer is that they are seeing your behavior, or what's on the surface. They don't see your good intentions, lofty ideals, and your heart. That's just reality. And so, aware of this reality, we should take time to consider what people see, determine how their view influences their ability to perform, and identify what, if anything, we need to change to bring out the best in those around us.

Behavior generally boils down to a good news/bad news story.

The Bad News

You can't control how people interpret your behavior. Their impression of you is filtered through their own experiences, values, culture, biases, personality, mood, and myriad other factors that influence how they decode the behavior they're seeing. In some cases, their view has been shaped by life events and relationships that took place long before you came on the scene and that have absolutely nothing to do with you. If you think that seems a bit unfair, you would be right.

Furthermore, it can all happen lightning fast. Traditional research suggests that within the first seven seconds of an encounter, people form an impression.[4] But if seven seconds seems like an absurdly small amount of time to make that all-important first impression, buckle up. A series of experiments by Princeton University psychologists Janine Willis and Alexander Todorov found that people can form an impression after being shown an image of another person's face for only 100 milliseconds, or one-tenth of a second.

---

4 Gibbons, Serenity. 2018. "You and your business have 7 seconds to make a first impressions: Here's How to succeed." *Forbes*, available at https://www.forbes.com/sites/serenitygibbons/2018/06/19/you-have-7-seconds-to-make-a-first-impression-heres-how-to-succeed/?sh=73acbb3c56c2. (Accessed March 2021).

Scientists have long known that people deemed more attractive get better treatment than those of us who lack movie star looks; people who appear competent (versus likeable) are more likely to be elected to public office; and lawbreakers who look more mature get harsher penalties than those with a more youthful appearance—but the Princeton researchers went a step further. Study participants were asked to view photos for very short time increments of 100 milliseconds, 500 milliseconds (half a second), and a whopping 1,000 milliseconds (a full second), and then judge the face they saw based on five traits: aggressiveness, attractiveness, competence, likeability, and trustworthiness. Their evaluations were then compared to a control group who were granted unlimited time to evaluate the same photos. Surprisingly, the tenth-of-a-second judgments were strongly correlated to those who had no time constraints and were similar to those who had taken slightly longer to form their judgment.[5]

Perhaps it's no surprise that study participants were most confident in their evaluation of the attractiveness of a person they had seen in a photo for only a split second, but trustworthiness was right there, as well. The implications of this research are both daunting and depressing. Only a tenth of a second to be labeled both ugly and shifty just doesn't seem fair!

There is hope, however. Researchers in this field suggest there is a series of small things you can do to improve the initial impression you make on people. An immediate smile—the international symbol

5 Janine Willis, and Alexander Todorov. 2006. "First Impressions: Making Up Your Mind After a 100-Ms Exposure to a Face." *Psychological Science* 17 (7): 592–98.

of altruism—can generate warm feelings and help people feel more connected to you. Standing or sitting with good posture and speaking slowly and clearly can shout confidence and intelligence. Good grooming and sharp dress certainly can't hurt either. But even then, the odds still would be stacked against us if that first impression was our only shot to influence people's perception.

The Good News

Now, for the good news. While most people form a first impression quickly, that instant evaluation can change over time—especially if there is an opportunity for a continuing relationship. Furthermore, the behavior upon which they base their judgments is malleable.

You can, and should, change your behavior if it isn't leading to the desired outcome.

Whether that outcome is how your team responds when you describe the mission or their willingness to share information with coworkers who are trying to push a project across the finish line, it's all influenced by your actions and how team members interpret them.

Over the last 20 years or so, these behaviors that impact others have been known as strengths. Landmark research by Gallup on strengths started a movement that has influenced talent development and self-help methods for years. I support much of the strength movement; however, I struggle to accept that your strengths are fixed and that success hinges on discovering your strengths so that you can anchor your life accordingly.

Don't misunderstand, please. It would be nice if success and satisfaction in life were achieved by simply identifying and cultivating our talents. It's an appealing idea, but probably not one that fully reflects reality. For example, I can't recall ever being assigned a task that I've had the option of saying, "Well, that's not really aligned with my strengths, so I'm going to pass." Instead, one must adapt to the demands of reality and accomplish the mission.

Since most of us work in the real world—as opposed to a mythical place where we can align each and every activity with our most potent strengths—perhaps we should think about strengths differently. I like to think of them as the behaviors we use to accomplish the mission when working with others. This way of thinking makes strengths like tools in a toolbox, with the goal to use the right one for the job. Of course, when people see us using the right tool—at least in their estimation—they respond favorably and join the effort by deploying some of their own tools.

I find the tool metaphor useful on a number of levels, perhaps because it's easy for me to relate. My wife, kids, and neighbors are all well aware that I'm not handy when it comes to household repairs. If it demands more skill than changing a lightbulb, I'm inclined to call in a professional. I'm a bit ashamed to admit this, but all of the tools I've acquired over the course of my adult life fit into a shoebox. This really limits what I can accomplish—and runs up quite a bill with my local handyman.

In stark contrast, my friend Ron is a tool guy. His garage is part Home Depot and part NAPA auto parts store. He seems to have every tool known to man and knows how to use them all. All I can do is gaze up at his wall of tools in wonder, as if I'm looking at a museum exhibit.

Ron's tools aren't on display to impress his mechanically inept neighbors. Rather, they are critical to his mission of maintaining his own cars and ably performing household repairs. In part, Ron enjoys the process of figuring out how things work and how to fix them, but he is able to take on a wide range of issues because he has a wide array of tools. He simply needs to choose the right tool for the job.

The same holds true for us. If you believe there are many possible ways to interact with a colleague, and you mindfully consider which would work best before charging in, you will likely get a good outcome. Those who rely on just a few strengths and apply them in every interaction are likely to miss the mark simply because the people, situation, and task at hand are constantly changing.

When people see you using the right tool, their confidence rises, they feel respected because you've taken the time to identify their needs, and they are more open to your guidance. And because people are always watching, your team will readily note your flexibility and tailored approach—even when the different tools are subtly applied.

Naming the different techniques you can showcase for people can be helpful as you consider which tool would be best for the job. Different strength assessments describe various behaviors differently, but ultimately, you'll just need to identify your particular tools, along with the when, where, why, and how of using them.

Some examples: If a member of your team is competent—even brilliant at times—but lacks self-confidence, you might want to show trust in them and confidence that they are capable of big things. Alternatively, if your manager asks you to take over a multimillion-dollar project that has been poorly managed, you might want to pump the brakes and carefully identify the most serious problems before diving in. Likewise, if you encounter a situation that creates an existential threat to the enterprise, you might need a strong "stop the presses" moment. Every situation and the people involved are different, so you need different approaches.

Putting different tools on display and allowing team members to see you making just-in-time adjustments lets people know that you are both aware of a situation and skillful enough to address it. They'll see a leader who doesn't apply a one-size-fits-all solution to a unique problem. People are always watching, so why not put on a good show?

Help People Understand What They're Seeing

People see your behavior—what's on the surface. They don't see what's driving that behavior, which lurks beneath the surface. That's simply unfair because your reasons or motives for behaving in a particular way are just as important—if not more so—than the behavior itself. Want proof? Have you ever said or done something that missed the mark? Perhaps the person misconstrued what was said and was upset, and you found yourself saying something like, "But that's not what I meant." We all have.

Being open about why you took certain actions gives others access to your thought process and the forces that shaped your decision. It also lets them correct the record or provide additional information if your logic is flawed.

Transparency provides perspective and invites feedback.

Letting others into your inner world also helps them see your humanity and forces them to consider their own motives. Otherwise, people often will see what they want to see, and their eyes may very well deceive them. Psychologists call this phenomenon "motivated perception" and it's been studied for years.[6]

One of the earliest studies was published in 1954 and was based on a 1951 football game between Dartmouth and Princeton. The outcome was disputed because many fans thought officials favored one team over the other. Researchers administered surveys to 324 fans—some students at Dartmouth and others, students at Princ-

---

6 Pogosyan, Marianna, July 9, 2019, "Why we see what we want to see." *Psychology Today*, available at https://www.psychologytoday.com/us/blog/between-cultures/201907/why-we-see-what-we-want-see. (Accessed March 2021).

eton—and discovered that they seemed to see different games. The happenings on the field that day were "real" to each person surveyed, but there were several variations on "real." Of course, anyone who has listened to contemporary sports radio probably isn't the least bit surprised at this finding, but it was some of the first scientific evidence that people viewing the same event can interpret what they see very differently.[7]

Other research suggests that people tend to see what they want to see. Participants in a series of five studies were shown a vague representation of a figure—one that could be seen as the number 13 or the letter B. Participants were told that if they perceived a particular image, they would be rewarded with a tasty refreshment; however, if they saw something else, they might be asked to drink a foul-smelling smoothie.[8] Well, it doesn't take a Ph.D. in psychology to deduce that people reported seeing what provided the reward.

These studies exemplify perceptual bias (we see what we want to see) and response bias (we inaccurately report information based on personal preferences). Both also explain how teammates tend to operate, reinforcing the notion that you need to clarify what's really happening—at least in relation to your behavior. Otherwise, they will fill in the blanks with their own story—good or bad—that not only may be untrue, but also may hinder efforts to accomplish the mission.

---

7   Hastorf, A. H., & Cantril, H. (1954), "They saw a game; a case study." *The Journal of Abnormal and Social Psychology*, 49(1), 129–134.

8   Balcetis, E., & Dunning, D. (2006), "See what you want to see: Motivational influences on visual perception," *Journal of Personality and Social Psychology*, 91(4), 612–625.

What are some practical ways to help people understand what they are seeing? Here are a few examples, but these lines must be delivered sincerely and with an open window to your thought process:

- Here's where I'm coming from...
- Let me explain why I responded that way...
- This was our rationale for the decision...
- I was influenced by...
- These data led me to...
- This is what I was trying to do...
- My intent was...
- We needed to change course because...
- Here's my understanding of the situation...

After any of these lead-ins (or one of your own design), simply explain your motivation for what you did or plan to do and, of course, how it relates to the mission.

Most people will appreciate the explanation. Some will understand and agree. Others may see it differently, but that's okay as long as those differences are handled as healthy opposition. Since you have just modeled open and candid communication, it may be time to invite feedback about what coworkers are seeing and how it sits with them. It's far better to be open about perceptions than to wrongly assume that everyone sees a situation the same.

People Can't Be What They Can't See

Nobel Prize laureate Dr. Albert Schweitzer taught that the most important ways to lead people are "by example, by example, and by example." Initially trained as a minister and theologian, Schweitzer wanted to do something more tangible to relieve suffering in the world, so he went to medical school. After becoming a surgeon, Schweitzer and his wife, a nurse, founded and ran a mission hospital in Gabon, on the west coast of Africa. He was also a gifted organist and gave concerts throughout Europe to fund his hospital.[9] The bottom line is, when Schweitzer saw tasks needing to be done, he did them, hopeful that others would do likewise.

Albert Schweitzer's life represents the power of example. In many ways, it's the essence of leadership. Leaders can't ask others to commit to the mission if they aren't committed themselves. The same holds true for making sacrifices, being accountable, and pursuing excellence. This is what makes hypocritical behavior so nauseating. It not only violates the very essence of leadership, but it damages credibility and diminishes mission importance. In my experience, when a leader's hypocrisy is revealed, innocent people are hurt, as well.

Example is also why it's so important to provide elevated platforms for women and people of color who have demonstrated excellence in their chosen fields. If we care about the future, applause for these successful people should not solely come from others in minority

---

9 The Norwegian Nobel Institute, "Albert Schweitzer facts," available at https://www. nobelprize.org/prizes/peace/1952/schweitzer/facts/ (Accessed March 2021).

groups. Instead, everyone should stand and cheer so that little boys and girls can see people who look like them rise to the pinnacles of power because of their positive contributions to the world. Unfortunately, without that visual, many cannot see what's possible, and their aspirations will align with their often-skewed field of vision.

I sometimes wonder what people see in my behavior, how it makes them think and feel, and how they will respond. Could I be the cause of some of my own problems because of the way others see me? The answers to these questions can guide the behavioral changes that, in turn, can lead to improved performance and better relationships—the reason you're reading. But let's dig a bit deeper into what people are seeing before prescribing particular changes.

reflection

Spend as much time as needed to answer the following questions about how people may see you as you interact with others and use your strengths to get things done. Be honest with yourself and try to think of specific examples as you respond to the prompts. Specific examples will provide deeper insight and help guide the adjustments you may want to make.

· Think about a typical day at work. What percentage of the day do your colleagues see you at your best? What percentage of time do they see you at far less than your best? What percentage of time do you wish that no one could see you at all?

- Think about a typical day at home—perhaps a Saturday, Sunday or other day off from work. What percentage of the day do your family and friends see you at your best? What percentage of time do they see you at far less than your best? What percentage of time do you wish that no one could see you at all?

- Compare your responses to questions 1 and 2. Are there major differences in your responses? If so, what does that tell you?

- Do you tend to approach most situations at work similarly or do you regularly adjust your approach based on the circumstances and people involved?

- Think of a recent example (i.e., within the last month) where you flexed and used a different approach based on your read of a situation. What was the response of your team? Did you think your flexibility hurt or helped in that situation?

- If you think about the strengths you use at work like tools in your relational toolbox, is your toolbox big or small?

- Who do you admire? Why are these people good role models?

- In what ways are you a good role model at work? In what ways are you a good role model at home?

action items

After reflecting on the questions above, choose one or more of the action items below to place on your to-do list this week or this month. Over time, work through the list. If you are consistent and make habits of these actions, you will likely see a good return on your investment.

- Ask a few friends or trusted colleagues how people see you. Encourage them to be completely candid—and don't get upset at them when they are!
- Try a different approach with a colleague with whom you've struggled to connect. For example, if a strong and as- sertive approach has gotten you nowhere, try being humbler and more curious. Keep adjusting your approach—and the way you use your tools—until you connect more positively with that person.
- Take the time to explain your decision or action to the people it impacted. You might use questions like these to guide your explanation: What logic guided your thinking? Were other forces at play of which others might not be

aware? What was the need for the change? What good intentions drove your response? Be as honest as you can, based on the situation.

- After observing another person's behavior that you initially find to be unsettling or disagreeable, ask them their reasons before judging them.

- Publicly acknowledge a colleague who you consider a role model. Emphasize the aspects of their work or character that you believe others should emulate. For a stretch assignment, do this for someone whose personality differs from yours.

additional reading

"A 3-Step Plan for Turning Weaknesses into Strengths," Joseph Grenny, January 26, 2017, *Harvard Business Review*, https://hbr.org/2017/01/a-3-step-plan-for-turning-weaknesses-into-strengths.

Atomic Habits: An Easy and Proven Way to Build Good Habits and Break Bad Ones, James Clear, Avery, 2018.

Change Anything: The New Science of Personal Success, Kerry Patterson, Joseph Grenny, David Maxfield, Ron McMillan, Al Switzler, 2011, Grand Central Publishing.

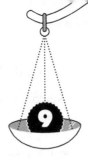

keep looking for the pony

the virtuous cycle that creates relationship

PRESIDENT RONALD REAGAN was known as "the great communicator" for good reason. In addition to delivering his conservative message with compelling clarity, his seemingly limitless repertoire of clever one-liners, stories, and jokes endeared him to friend and foe alike. His loyal staff never quite knew when he would call on his sense of humor to break the ice, but they trusted his judgment and timing.

One of the best-known Reagan jokes was about a family who had twin boys with opposite dispositions. One child was an extreme pessimist, finding risk and darkness in every situation. The boy's brother was an optimist to the core—no matter the situation, he remained bright and cheerful. As word got out about the boys and their differences, researchers at the local university asked their parents if they would allow the boys to participate in a study.

The parents agreed, and on the day of the study, the family arrived to find two separate rooms. The pessimistic boy was taken into a brightly lit room filled with brand new toys of every variety.

The scientists told the boy that he could play with any of the toys for as long as he wanted—even take them home. The little boy immediately became overwhelmed and began to sob: "There are so many; how can I choose? And I'll probably break them anyway!"

Meantime, his brother was ushered into a dark, smelly roomed filled to the ceiling with horse manure. The child psychologists observed through a one-way window, anxious to see how the optimistic boy would respond to such awful conditions. Incredibly, he began jumping and playing in the manure. At times, he even rooted around in the nasty stuff, scooping up fistfuls of it. Fearing they had triggered some sort of breakdown in the boy, the baffled scientists rushed into the room.

When they got his attention, they asked, "What in the world are you doing?"

"With all of this manure," the gleeful boy responded, "there's got to be a pony in here somewhere!"[1]

As the crowd laughed raucously at Reagan's masterfully delivered story, the president would make a point neatly tied to the day's message—perhaps something about the manure he had to dig through in Washington. In our case, the point is that curiosity is critical to finding the good stuff. More importantly, it's the starting point for a virtuous cycle that leads to notably diverse organizations staffed with people who sincerely want to work well together.

---

1 Robinson, Peter, *How Ronald Reagan Changed My Life*, New York: Harper Collins, 2003.

Through the mission-first lens, curiosity invites us to learn and creatively explore innovative ways to get the job done. At different points in your career, you may even feel like the two little boys in Reagan's story. There are times when there are so many good and interesting opportunities that it's difficult to decide what to take on first. I genuinely hope that's where you are now. Other times, it may feel as though you're standing where the dump truck dropped off the load of manure and much of it landed on you. Surprisingly, in both situations, the proper response is the same: Be curious. The right question to ask is: "What can I learn from this situation?" The next question follows closely on the heels of the first: "Is there a better way?"

Through the people-always lens, we can sharpen the focus on developing relationships with people who are unlike us and toward whom we may even have a negative bias. Admittedly, bias is a tough topic and one that many are hesitant to address. However, my goal in the next few pages is not to pass judgment nor label anyone as bad or good by invoking moral code. Rather, just as in the preceding pages, we should focus on creating an environment that fosters seamless teamwork, thereby elevating performance and getting the mission accomplished. Most importantly, we will use two positive mindsets—curiosity and empathy—to bust biases and help everyone build more productive relationships.

The Virtuous Cycle

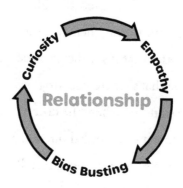

The Case for Curiosity

We've all heard the idiom, "Curiosity killed the cat." Of course, it's generally used to stop people—especially children, who don't want to see harm come to the kitty—from asking unwanted questions.

Albert Einstein never bought into it, though. In an interview published in *Life* magazine on May 2, 1955, he said:

"The important thing is not to stop questioning. Curiosity has its own reason for existing. One cannot help but be in awe when he contemplates the mysteries of eternity, of life, of the marvelous structure of reality. It is enough if one tries merely to comprehend a little of this mystery every day."[2]

No one has been better than Einstein at unpacking the mysteries of the universe. Yet, even this brilliant man was known to be

---

2 Einstein, Albert (1955, May 2) quoted in *Life.*

self-centered and unkind. In a series of letters between Einstein and his first wife, Mileva Maric, between 1897 and 1903, researchers found a list of absurdly harsh conditions Einstein required if their relationship were to continue. Demands that she stop talking and leave the room immediately upon being told to do so, along with unfailing attention to household chores, do not paint a flattering picture of an enlightened man. Einstein asked for a divorce from Mileva in 1916. After his second wife, Elsa, died in 1936, Einstein wrote that his life was better without her, admitting that he just wasn't good with people and preferred to live alone.[3]

How could this man who most consider a secular saint in the world of science have been so callous? So devoid of empathy? Apparently, he had insatiable curiosity about time and space but didn't care to understand the people in his life. We might say that Einstein was always "mission first" but people were never a priority. We can't be that way, and contemporary research about the benefits of curiosity in business explains why.

Harvard Business School professor Francesca Gino headed up research that identified four major benefits of curiosity in the workplace. She found that curiosity compels leaders and teams to make better decisions, innovate and pursue creative solutions, have less

---

3 *Open Culture*, December 30, 2013, "Albert Einstein imposes on his first wife a cruel list of marital demands." Available at https://www.openculture.com/2013/12/albert-einstein-imposes-on-his-first-wife-a-cruel-list-of-marital-demands.html (Accessed March 2021).

conflict, and communicate better.[4] Let's unpack each and place it in the context of mission first, people always.

Fewer errors. We make fewer mistakes that impact our results and relationships when we're curious. Curiosity reduces the risk that we'll fall prey to confirmation bias, or the tendency to focus on information that confirms our beliefs rather than looking for evidence that we may be wrong. Curiosity also invites us to reject stereotypes. Instead of painting groups with broad, negative strokes, curiosity invites us to get to know people as individuals—up close and personal. A curious desire to know people is the genesis of relationship.

Greater productivity, innovation, and positivity. Some no-nonsense leaders might be tempted to see curiosity as a distraction; however, there is evidence to the contrary. INSEAD professor Spencer Harrison and colleagues found that curiosity leads to greater productivity in a study that looked at artisans selling products online. Using an assessment to measure the degree of curiosity, the researchers found that even a one-point increase in the artisans' curiosity scores equaled as much as a 34% gain in productivity, as measured by the number of items they made and put up for sale online.

Harrison and his colleagues also studied the productivity of workers in call centers, where the work tends to be highly structured and people come and go constantly. Employees who displayed greater curiosity were more likely to uncover customers' needs, offer creative solutions to address them, and help raise customer satisfaction ratings.

---

4 Gino, Francesca, September-October 2018. "The business case for curiosity," *Harvard Business Review*, available at https://hbr.org/2018/09/the-business-case-for-curiosity (Accessed March 2021).

In another study led by Professor Gino's team, employees from varying industries were sent twice-weekly text messages at the beginning of their work day that invited them to ask questions or pursue topics about which they were curious—or seek to understand something they might normally take for granted. In short, they were encouraged to ask more "why" questions and to approach their work accordingly. Other study participants (the control group) were also sent texts, but the messages were related to specific tasks on the to-do list that day.

After only four weeks, the group that was encouraged to ask more "why" questions was found to offer more constructive suggestions and creative ideas for solving pressing problems. In short, they added value. Other academic studies have shown that curiosity is associated with better job performance and fewer defensive responses in stressful situations. The evidence in support of curiosity is mounting.

Better communication and improved teamwork. When people truly want to hear the perspectives of others, they more willingly engage in conversation. On the other hand, collaboration and creative problem solving suffer when people are purely focused on transactional communication—getting only the information needed to accomplish a task with no interest in anything more. Often, a conversation can become a dynamic and practical interaction with the simple question, "What are you trying to do?"

Professor Gino again studied this phenomenon, this time in a program for government executives at the Harvard Kennedy School.

As a precursor to a team activity to measure performance, some study participants were assigned group activities designed to stimulate their curiosity, while other groups were given more mundane tasks. Observers noted that participants who entered the performance-oriented activity with a heightened sense of curiosity more freely shared information and listened more intently to their teammates. This helped them solve the problems more efficiently and achieve higher scores than less-curious groups.

Reduced conflict. Earlier, we touched on how we deal with conflict when we feel something important to us is being attacked. Each of us responds to these perceived attacks differently, but we are far less likely to feel threatened when we're approached by someone who is sincerely trying to understand our point of view. That stance—the desire to understand—often turns a potential conflict into healthy opposition or genuine collaboration.

Given these benefits, it's only logical to think everyone would want a seat on the curiosity bandwagon. Again, Professor Harrison at INSEAD, supported by research scientists at Survey Monkey, helps us see why this isn't the case. In part, disparity exists between how well executives think they're fostering curiosity in employees and what employees actually experience. While misaligned expectations are an ongoing problem, it's important to understand how that relates to curiosity.

The researchers surveyed 23,000 people—about 16,000 individual contributors, 1,500 C-suite leaders, and 5,500 midlevel managers across a variety of industries. They found that 83% of the executive-level leaders believed they actively encouraged curiosity, yet only 52% of individual contributors felt empowered to embrace curiosity and explore. There was also misalignment regarding the perceived value of curiosity. C-level leaders believed it was rewarded by salary growth, while just 16% of individual contributors agreed. An overwhelming 81% of individual contributors believed curiosity made no difference in their compensation.[5] In other words, why bother?

If leaders sincerely believe that curiosity is valuable and want to encourage it, they must find more active ways to embed and embrace it in the daily rhythms of work. Employees also need to believe they are empowered to pursue interests beyond a daily task list and also that there is something in it for them—a pony, perhaps?

exercise

Still not convinced of the value of curiosity? Perhaps you're thinking it sounds good, but you don't know how to do it—especially when interacting with new faces. Blame it on your introversion or a general lack of social skills, but curiosity is easier said than done. My hope is that you will be willing to do your own social science re-

5   Harrison, Spence, Pinkus, Erin, and Cohen, Jon. September 20, 2018. "Research: 83% of executives say they encourage curiosity. Just 52% of employees agree." *Harvard Business Review.* Available at https://hbr.org/2018/09/research-83-of-executives-say-they-encourage-curiosity-just-52-of-employees-agree (Accessed March 2021).

search. No academic appointment is required, although the research conditions may remind you of your college days. I call my experiment Life of the Party.

Step 1: Get yourself invited to a party. Almost any party will do, but the gathering must include several people you don't know.

Step 2: Spend part of your time—up to an hour—expressing absolutely no curiosity. Only respond to questions with one- or two-word answers and, whatever you do, don't ask any questions in return; try to find a place you can sit alone and as far as possible from other guests, and avoid meeting anyone new. In short, pretend you are socially awkward and have no interpersonal skills, or you could play an arrogant jerk who is too good to associate with the likes of this party crowd. In short, choose the shoe that fits best—in the service of scientific research, of course.

Step 3: Assess whether you're enjoying yourself at the party. Are you engaged? Would you prefer to be someplace else? Is the needle on your internal fun meter even moving? Make some notes. By the way, pulling out a notebook at a cocktail party is a surefire way to sell the socially awkward, nerdy character you were trying to develop.

You've now completed the first half of our informal experiment. Let's move along to the second half to see if you get different results.

Step 4: Find someone you don't know and begin asking questions. Don't be weird and keep everything respectful, but apart from that, almost any questions will do. You might start with some old standards: "How do you know the host?" "Where are you from?"

"How long have you lived in this area?" "What do you do for a living?" "Tell me about your family..." The keys to success in this phase of the experiment are to be sincere, be conversational, go with the flow, and stay curious.

Step 5: After a few minutes, find someone else to engage. Use the same technique, and feel free to laugh and enjoy the conversation. Keep repeating until it's time to go home.

Step 6: Conduct an honest self-evaluation: Did you enjoy yourself more in the first half of the party or the second? My hypothesis is that you had a far better time when you engaged with people and demonstrated curiosity. They probably liked you a lot better, too, which could lead to more party invitations—and opportunities to repeat the experiment to substantiate your findings.

You might think my experiment is a bit silly, but it describes life at work, as well. If we engage people and get to know them, we are more likely to enjoy our working hours with them. However, if we remain aloof, limiting our interactions to those with whom we have a formal reporting relationship, the workplace is likely to be less interesting and your impact as a leader will suffer.

Inspiring Curiosity in Others

Whether it was the scholarly literature, your own life experience, or a little party-themed research, let's assume you get it. You recognize that continuing to dig will yield something good—perhaps new or better ways to accomplish the mission, or techniques to bring out the best in people. So, how do you convince others to buy in, too?

The best way to inspire the behavior you want is to model it. If you want people to be curious about the work they're doing or the people they're doing it with, be curious yourself. Our research at the party proved it's not difficult with the right frame of mind and a few questions at your disposal.

A positive mindset is essential. Curiosity works best if you don't have an agenda, you're open to whatever comes your way, and you resist passing judgment. Sincerity is also critical—everyone will know if you're just going through the motions—but it's much easier to be sincere if you truly believe you're going to benefit in some way from the conversation. Finally, be a good listener. Don't interrupt, and show your engagement with eye contact and body language.

Now that your mindset is right, you're ready to begin opening others' minds to find the good stuff inside. Here's another simple experiment—and this time, you don't even need to go to a party. What do you **think** when you're told what to do? Be honest. You sometimes resist. You may shut down. You want to get away. You question whether that person is authorized to tell you what to do. You think about how you can accomplish the task quickly to get that person off your back. These and other less-than-positive thoughts can create a pretty dark scene inside your brain.

A better method is to stop telling people what to do and ask more questions. It's a great way to model curiosity and to engage people more productively in the moment. Sincere questions invite people to lower their guard and engage their brains.

Here are some general examples of questions that may inspire others:

- How do you think we can best accomplish the task?
- What's your recommendation?
- What was your goal? What were you trying to accomplish?
- How did you feel about what happened?
- What's the best course of action now?
- What are some other options?
- What did you learn?
- How will you do it differently next time?
- Any ideas about what went wrong?

Please note that none of the questions begin with "why"— to avoid sounding accusatory in moments when emotions are running a bit hot.

Again, to get the most out of curiosity-based conversations, don't have an agenda. If you do, most people will quickly recognize it and feel manipulated. When savvy people recognize they're being manipulated, they become guarded, and any hopes of creating a team culture based on openness, honesty, and curiosity will quickly fade. The only agenda you should have is a sincere desire to learn.

Don't ask questions when either person involved is upset or angry. Some people find it difficult to think clearly and articulate their thoughts in a heated moment, while others tend to say things they may later regret. It's better to let all involved cool off, gather their thoughts, and then calmly talk it over.

Finally, and this goes back to the right mindset, ask curious questions from the heart. Be sincere. Have a desire to learn where the other person is coming from, because that's the path to empathy.

Empathy as a Performance Accelerator

More and more over the past few years, my Fortune 500 clients are recognizing empathy as a vital leadership competency. The Center for Creative Leadership, a highly respected think tank and leadership training organization, looked at data from 6,731 managers in 38 countries to see if there was a positive correlation between job performance and the degree of empathy they displayed. These empathetic managers not only achieved better results, but were also considered better leaders by executives in their organizations. Not surprisingly, their subordinates also gave them high marks.[6]

Simply put, empathy is the ability to see the world through another person's eyes—to imagine yourself in that situation and feel what they're feeling. This emotional connectedness breeds compassion that makes leaders less judgmental, more approachable, and refreshingly willing to meet people where they are.

---

6 Center for Creative Leadership (n.d.). "The Importance of Empathy in the Workplace." Available at https://www.ccl.org/articles/leading-effectively-articles/empathy-in-the-workplace-a-tool-for-effective-leadership/. (Accessed April 8, 2021).

Empathy and sympathy should not be confused. Sympathy is characterized by feelings of pity, but with no real understanding of what that person is experiencing. It can actually create feelings of superiority that cripple relationships, because it's difficult to feel connected where there is inequity.

One of the best-known examples of the transformative power of empathy is provided by Charles Dickens' *A Christmas Carol*. The familiar story tells how mean-spirited and miserable old Ebenezer Scrooge, whose disdainful treatment of employee Bob Cratchit was widely known, is confronted by Christmas ghosts of the past, present, and future. They teach him the power of seeing the world from other perspectives and lead him to live the remainder of his life with compassion, generosity, and a more favorable disposition. Fortunately, we don't have to be confronted by Marley's ghost and his scared-straight routine to embrace empathy.

We embrace empathy because it makes us more human.

When we experience our own humanity more fully, we treat others with respect and demand dignity for all. In short, it makes us better. I doubt that anyone reading this would disagree, yet we regularly miss opportunities to experience the benefits of empathy, especially when it comes to the people who are most unlike us.

Almost any difference presents both an opportunity and challenge for empathy, and differences certainly abound in today's diverse workplace. A colleague may look different, speak with a foreign accent, or embrace a lifestyle that you would not choose. Regardless, these are the moments when we can sincerely try to understand that person's experience by drawing closer to them, or we can keep a polite distance and do our best to tolerate their presence in **our** world. I've discovered that hearing another person's story helps me to make the right decision.

Personal stories have great power to spark empathy. The seemingly never-ending violence by police against African-American men made me want to draw closer to some of my students and friends to hear their stories. Because I teach in a doctoral program, my students tend to be mature adults with advanced degrees who, in most cases, have found success in work and life. Yet, my heart ached as I heard one of them describe how he had been pulled over multiple times by police and twice removed from his car at gunpoint, handcuffed, and questioned because he "fit the description" of someone who had committed a crime in the area. The description: black male.

I've also spent time with law-enforcement professionals to hear their stories. From local cops to federal agents, many have harrowing tales of their own. Recently, I spoke with a 14-year homicide investigator who has seen inhumanity at its worst—up close and personal. From gangland slayings to serial killers, he thought he had seen it all. Then, he was chosen to lead his city's sex crimes unit, where the horror continued.

Because some people are intent on doing terrible things to others, he goes to work every day, intent on bringing evildoers to justice. He sees it as a righteous calling. And I'm grateful he's there.

Asked what could be done about racial tension, his answer was immediate: "I wish we could just talk to each other. More importantly, I wish we would all listen." It's simple advice with broad application. What if people had sincere dialogue with those who were different and allowed their stories to seep into their souls? What would the impact be?

Bias Busting

By definition, bias is a prejudice for or against one thing, one person, or one group. It's a cognitive shortcut to making decisions that, in some cases, can be quite useful. For example, my wife has a bias toward healthy, organic foods. Therefore, she makes decisions while shopping and preparing meals that are in our family's dietary best interests. Unfortunately, many biases are based on stereotypes and lies rather than true understanding.

This is especially true of inaccurate labels placed on groups of people. Group-based biases are far too plentiful, with each capable of doing serious harm. Sometimes, we're aware of these negative biases and can challenge ourselves to overcome them. Other times, deeply imbedded biases escape conscious detection and become implicit. Whether rooted in current cultural undertones or things we learned as children, they're there—and sometimes they're really ugly. In the context of the workplace, these filters can hurt both people and performance.

The world has come a long way towards confronting longstanding prejudice. Some of these bias-busting activities have even caused us to consider the existence of unconscious biases that can stealthily erode the culture and productivity of our organizations.

Unconscious biases can be fairly innocuous (e.g., Google engineers designed a YouTube video uploading app that only worked properly for right-handed people[7]) to clear examples of discrimination like those illustrated in the results of a two-year study by professor Sonia Kang and her colleagues that found job interview invitations were more likely when African-Americans "whitened" their resumes.[8] These kinds of biases are destructive at all levels.

There are no easy answers to the problem of "we don't know what we don't know" about unconscious bias; however, a good place to start is getting to know the people on your path well so that you no longer see them as "types" or as a representative of a group. It's easy to dislike people from a distance, but much more difficult with

7 Bock, Laszlo, Welle, Brian. September 25, 2014. "You don't know what you don't know: How our unconscious minds undermine the workplace." Available at https://blog.google/inside-google/life-at-google/you-dont-know-what-you-dont-know-how/ (Accessed April 12, 2021).

8 Kang, Sonia K., Katherine A DeCelles, Tilcsik András, and Sora Jun. 2016. "Whitened Résumés: Race and Self-Presentation in the Labor Market." *Administrative Science Quarterly* 61 (3): 469–502.

someone you know well. I've found that when you move closer to see others more clearly, hear their voices, and understand the challenges they face, even the hardest of hearts tend to soften.

I think this is what President Lincoln had in mind when he gave himself some advice about dealing with his political adversaries.

Lincoln famously said, "I don't like that man. I need to get to know him better."

Knowing people creates a connection that moves us closer to collaboration, communication, and working better together.

The best way to bust a bias and build a relationship is the same. Both occur when we're sincerely curious about people, avoid judgmental thoughts, and develop empathy. I like to think of this as the virtuous cycle of relationship building—and one of the primary ways we balance people and performance. It's what leaders do on a daily basis and what aspiring leaders should learn to do well. Relationship is both a mindset and skill set, and this book provides numerous examples of how to do both with greater effect. Take the next step by working through the following reflection questions and action items.

reflection

Spend as much time as needed to answer these questions about how you have used curiosity to reduce bias and build relationships. Be honest with yourself and try to think of specific examples, which will provide deeper insight and help to guide the adjustments you may want to make.

- Thinking back, have you considered curiosity a major benefit and contributor to your success or did you view asking questions as something that would just slow you down?

- Are you inclined to accept the way things are and work within the system or do you want to understand **why** things are as they are and potentially find a better way?

- When you review the four business benefits of curiosity from Dr. Gino's research, which one resonates most for you based on your experience? How have you seen it serve the mission or the people who have come together to accomplish it?

- Do you have a positive mindset for curiosity (PMC) or does your mindset need some work?

- How have you encouraged someone else to be curious this week?

- What are some of your conscious biases? How do they help or hurt your leadership?
- Is there someone in your sphere of influence you need to get to know better—perhaps because you dislike them?

action items

After reflecting on the preceding questions, choose one or more of the action items below to place on your to-do list this week or this month. Over time, work through the list. If you are consistent and make habits of these actions, you will likely see a good return on your investment.

- Learn everything you can about a product, process, or person in your organization that you presently know little about. Let your curiosity fuel questions and inspire you to think differently about your subject. When finished, consider whether it was an energizing or deflating experience. What new ideas did it inspire? Do it again to verify your findings.
- Ask at least three curiosity questions (provided earlier in the chapter) each day for a week. The following week, make it four questions per day. At the end of two weeks, assess how people are responding to you at work. Do they appear

to be more willing to engage with you? Do they seek you out for advice or consultation? How did your mindset change as you engaged with people during the course of your experiment?

· Become more intentional about hearing the stories of all of your direct reports or peers. Where are they from? What was the career path that brought them to their current role? When are they most engaged at work? What are their aspirations at work and beyond? Assess whether your feelings toward that person change as result of your conversation(s).

· Encourage someone (or several people) on your team to pursue an interest that they've been curious about but just haven't had a chance to explore. You can decide whether the interest has to be directly related to work or they can expand the horizon.

· Identify three people with whom you want to develop a stronger relationship over the next year. Rate your progress on a monthly or quarterly basis.

additional reading

Biased: Uncovering the Hidden Prejudice that Shapes What We See, Think, and Do, Jennifer L. Eberhardt, Penguin Books, 2020.

Cracking the Curiosity Code: The Key to Unlocking Human Potential, Diane Hamilton, Gatekeeper Press, 2018.

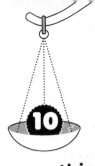

the one thing

it all comes down to relationships

B Y DESIGN, PREVIOUS chapters have taken a topical approach to discussing factors that affect your ability to accomplish the mission and bring out the best in your team. Along the way, I trust that you recognized how both the mission and the people pursuing it must be managed with precise balance, or the disparity will lead to problems. In fact, the message of this book is that lasting success can only be achieved when mission and people abide in harmony.

We've covered a variety of ways by which this can be accomplished, although I make no claims that these are the only effective methods. Everything I did offer, however, is necessary to build high-performing teams. It also seems only right, especially in the final chapter, to integrate these distinct elements and direct them all to a single focal point. In other words, I wanted to boil it all down into the "one thing you should remember."

What I've discovered is that better results, stronger teams, more impactful careers, and happier lives all come down to relationships. We have loosely used an old-fashioned balance scale as a metaphor to describe the delicate equilibrium a manager must find between the task at hand and the need to take care of the people working to accomplish it. A huge key are the relationships that teammates have with each other—and especially the leader—that serve as building blocks for extraordinary results.

Narrowing down the elements of success to one thing is risky. Some critics will rationally argue that it's overly simplistic to say that developing better relationships can put you on the fast track to unbridled success. In some ways, they might be right. I suppose that depends on how one defines success.

If we're honest, many of us are still trying to settle on our own definition of success. For me, it has changed over the years. Early in my career, it was about the proverbial ladder to the top. It didn't matter which ladder or where the top might be—I just wanted to get there fast. Now, things are different and my mission has changed. The ladders have been traded in for the intense satisfaction that comes from helping others dream big and accomplish missions that make the world better, while equipping people to grow, develop, and become difference makers in their own right. I'm finding more and more people who feel that way, as well.

Billy Furlong owns Aloha Landscape, a successful builder of beautiful outdoor spaces in Southern California. I got to know Billy and his crew during the three months or so it took them to transform our property into a wonderful alfresco space to enjoy with family and friends. Billy coined the term "blank canvas" because it was the kindest term he could summon to describe the barren wasteland of dirt, rocks, and weeds that my wife and I placed in his care. Because I was working from home on this book, I got to know Billy and interacted with his crew daily.

Near the end of the project, I complimented Billy on the team he had assembled. They were all incredibly diligent, attentive to every detail, courteous, respectful, and genuinely nice guys. And although Spanish was their first language, most spoke English well enough for me to interact with them and share a laugh or two. Over time, I found myself looking forward to seeing them each day—partly because I so craved human contact after a year of COVID19-related restrictions.

Billy responded to my compliment by sharing some stories that revealed his philosophy of leadership. He told me about Hector, his team lead. Hector is a small, wiry guy who one minute would be balancing a tall stack of tiles as he tightroped across a roof, and the next moment he'd be knee deep in a muddy trench. He seemed to be everywhere, but no matter where he was, he wore a big smile.

Billy explained that he met Hector as a skinny 18-year-old standing in front of a store with other day laborers looking for work. Billy had a backbreaking project on his agenda and Hector looked qualified to lend a hand, so he invited him to jump into the truck. Seeing how hard Hector worked that first day, Billy invited him back for the next day's job, and the next, and the next. That continued until Billy made him a full-time employee with full documentation.

What Hector lacked in experience, he made up for with an eagerness to learn and the willingness to try new things. Billy, always the patient teacher, would show Hector how to perform one of the many tasks associated with the landscape business, and Hector would soon master it. Twenty-two years later, Hector has a wife and three children, and there isn't much related to landscaping or construction that he doesn't know how to do.

After finishing Hector's story of the American dream, Billy said, "If you like that one, let me tell you Gilbert's story." I knew Gilbert. He was the foreman who helped Billy run the business and had communicated with me a few times about the financial side of the project. He had also stopped by on several occasions to inspect his guys' work.

Billy explained that only seven years ago, Gilbert had blown up his marriage, lost a successful business and was homeless as a result of addictions. Gilbert found his way to church, where he experienced a dramatic conversion that helped him kick his bad habits. Supported by new friends and a church family, the newly transformed Gilbert needed to get back on his feet financially and was willing to work hard to get there. One of Gilbert's church friends and an Aloha employee asked his boss, Billy, to give Gilbert a chance.

Billy knew within a few days that he had made a good decision in hiring Gilbert. Billy said, "I could literally see him sweating out the poison that had circulated in his system for so long, but he just kept going." Over time, Gilbert became a leader in the field and shared that he had some computer and business management skills that might help Aloha reach its mission.

Gilbert is now Billy's right-hand-man, involved in every aspect of the business and fully committed to his work. He and his new wife also serve in his church's food ministry every Sunday—because Gilbert has a pretty good handle on what grace is all about at this point. Later, as Gilbert shared his testimony with me, I couldn't help but think about all the people who were placed in Gilbert's path to become part of his story. In other words, relationships—and the grace of God—made the difference in Gilbert's life.

Before Billy had any idea that I would include his story in a book, I asked him to explain his philosophy of leadership. His response was not surprising, yet compelling: "I just believe in giving guys a chance. I get to know them—ask about their families and what's important to them. I make sure they know how to do their jobs and that each of them is important to what we do." Apparently, it works. Aloha has been in business for nearly 30 years and has hundreds of happy customers. And Billy... his success is not only measured in financial terms, but in the lives of the men he has "given a chance" and who have contributed to Aloha's mission. In fact, Billy might even say that his ultimate mission is giving guys like Hector and Gilbert that chance.

Your circumstances may be much different. But, while you may not have opportunities to turn day laborers into committed, long-term employees, or to grow a formerly homeless addict to your second-in-command, the leadership principle is the same. Leaders who build strong relationships are better positioned to accomplish the mission—no matter what that might be.

Think back to the "Getting Started" chapter of this book, where I asked you to consider the **best** and the **worst** leaders of your career. Since the main criterion for each list was that you had a personal connection with that person, perhaps you considered that to be daily or almost-daily contact. That allowed us to exclude some of the usual suspects, like historical figures and others you have only read about or seen on television. It also suggests that you had a relationship with each person on your list, be it good or bad.

Now that we're almost to the end of the book, think about what made those leaders the best and worst. With the best, you very likely had a clear sense of your mission and the important role you played. You probably also felt that your best leader took the time to get to know you, invested in you, and gave you a voice. Your ideas mattered to that leader, and it was safe to express them.

The team you were on at the time also was certain to actively communicate, collaborate, and use their individual strengths to complement group efforts. Everyone had an important role to play, but you probably had a fair amount of fun, too. Ineffective leaders, on the other hand, allow the people around them to build siloes, withhold information, and pull in different directions. There's usually so much backstabbing and badmouthing going on that there's little room for fun.

The difference should be clear. That was the past; this is now. What kind of leader will you be? If a colleague picks up this book five years from now, will you be on their **best** list?

Leadership is about getting things done— sometimes under the most difficult of circumstances—and building relationships along the way.

As we've learned, the two go hand in hand, and you can't have one without the other. Performance and people, in balance, is the only surefire way to succeed in business and in life. That balance, as precarious as it may be, can only occur when you're investing in relationships. It all comes down to that.

reflection

Spend as much time as needed to answer the following questions about how you leverage your relationships at work to improve performance. Be honest with yourself and try to think of specific examples, which will provide deeper insight and help to guide any adjustments you may want to make.

- Who is the one person in your professional life with whom you would like to build a more productive relationship? What might be the impact on your team's performance? Would a better relationship with that person improve your career prospects?
- Looking back, how have your relationships helped or hurt your career?
- If you could turn back time, who are some of the people in your professional life with whom you would do things differently relationally? How would you interact with them differently today?
- What are two or three big ideas you're taking away after reading this book?
- Who are the two or three people in your circle of influence who might benefit from this book or some of the suggested developmental readings?

action items

After reflecting on the questions above, choose one or more of the action items below to place on your to-do list for this week or this month. Over time, work through the list. If you are consistent and make habits of these actions, you will likely see a good return on your investment.

- Identify the specific actions you can take to improve a relationship with one key stakeholder. What will you do first? When will you begin?
- Share a copy of this book with a few up-and-coming folks in your organization. Perhaps they are aspiring leaders, members of your team, or peers. As you share the book, also share one or two positive points from it.
- Give someone a chance by investing in them. Even though they may be an unlikely candidate, make an effort to bring out the best in them and see what happens.

additional reading

Dare to Lead, Brene Brown, Random House, 2018.

Multipliers: How the Best Leaders Make Everyone Smarter, Liz Wiseman, Harper Business, 2010.

Mindset: The New Psychology of Success, Carol. S. Dweck, Ballentine Books, 2016.

What's Next?

Now that you're at the end of the book, the question you should be asking yourself is, "What's next?" Along the way, I hope you were entertained, challenged, and even inspired. Most importantly, I hope you learned something that will make you a better leader or teammate. But this won't happen if you set the book aside, never to consider its ideas again. Instead, consider taking the following next steps that will help you sustain and apply what you learned:

- If you haven't yet worked through all the reflection questions at the end of each chapter, go back and spend some time thinking through your responses. It's even better if you take the time to write out your responses in a journal. Journaling helps you organize your thoughts; set and achieve goals, and improve your writing skills. It has also been demonstrated to reduce stress and boost creativity.
- Work on at least one action item each week. Let people who care about you know what you're doing because they would, undoubtedly, like to help. Examples are your manager, a mentor, or an executive coach. Trustworthy friends or your spouse would be great choices, too.
- Invite others to join you on your journey. Ask members of your team to read the book and set aside one day a week—perhaps over lunch or a virtual happy hour—to talk through the reflection questions in each chapter.

- Connect with me on LinkedIn at https://www.linkedin. com/in/drmichaellpatterson. That's where I'll post articles, blogs, or opportunities.

- Invest in training that brings these ideas to life. Whether self-paced eLearning or with a facilitator and group of people, practicing the behaviors associated with a mission first, people always culture is always helpful. Please contact me at mike@drmikepatterson.com to discuss your options.

- Keep reading. There are many great books and articles on a wide array of topics that will support and encourage you along the way. Remember, leadership and continuous learning must always go together.

- Finally, if you enjoyed the book and think others might benefit as well, please tell someone. One of the best ways to do this is by posting a review on Amazon or one of the other sites that sell the book. Just a few words from you could be enough to start someone else on this journey. And wouldn't the world be a better place if everyone had a mission first, people always perspective?

appendix

exercise

Calculate the Cost of Conflict

U SE THIS SIMPLE worksheet to consider just how much conflict may be costing you and your organization. Even though some of the numbers you use are likely to be estimates, the exercise will help you get a sense for how much you could save if you could prevent or better manage interpersonal conflict.

Getting Started

Think about a recent conflict in your organization that you believe negatively impacted performance. Briefly describe the situation here and identify the primary people involved. If you feel like adding a little memorable flair, you can name the conflict, as well (i.e., "The Thrilla in Manila"). These names may help you keep your conflicts straight if you want to do this exercise multiple times.

Description:

_____

_____

_____

_____

People involved (don't forget management and HR professionals):

_____

_____

_____

Time:

_____

_____

_____

Now that you've identified everyone involved, estimate how many hours these people spent dealing with the conflict. Include the wasted time associated with people gossiping with peers, complaining to managers or HR, pouting, etc., and any absences directly related to the conflict. If your team was working from home when the conflict occurred, it may be more difficult to calculate wasted time, but make your best guess.

Line A: Number of hours _____

Estimate an average hourly wage for the people involved. Don't forget to "fully load" that hourly wage by including the cost of health insurance and benefits. If you're completely stumped, make an educated guess. According to the U.S. Bureau of Labor Statistics, the average hourly wage in January 2020 was $28.44.

Line B: Average hourly wage _____

Find the total time-related costs by multiplying lines **A** and **B** (**A** X **B**).

Line C: Total time-related costs _____

Turnover

Did anyone end up leaving the organization because of the conflict? Were they replaced? If so, estimate the cost of replacing each lost employee by multiplying their annual salary (estimate, if necessary) by 1.5. This is simply an estimate intended to consider recruiting costs, the time needed to train and ramp up the new employee, etc. The actual cost is probably much higher—especially if it is a senior level position—but let's be conservative.

If you are aware of lost business associated with turnover (a departing sales rep took her book of business to a different employer), feel free to include that amount, as well.

Line D: Turnover costs _____

HR / Legal

Did the conflict become so contentious that HR or Legal had to get involved? Did someone complain to the Equal Employment Opportunity Commission or union? Did anyone file a lawsuit that had to be defended or settled? This information may be difficult to gather unless you were directly involved in the case, but as a point of reference, the average hourly rate for an employment attorney in California is $350 (for smaller firms or less experienced attorneys) to $475 and higher (large firms or more experienced attorneys). Even if your company has in-house legal counsel, many cases are settled in order to avoid the costs and risks of protracted litigation.

Line E: HR / Legal costs _____

Performance

Did the organization lose a deal or miss a deadline as a result of the conflict? Did mistakes have to be fixed? Did a product or process need to be redesigned?

Line F: Performance costs _____

Reputation

Did your organization's reputation suffer as a result of the conflict? Perhaps some of the people involved took to social media to bash the company or left scathing comments on Glassdoor.com that will hamper efforts to attract top candidates. Again, it's likely difficult to estimate these costs, but in some of the worst cases, companies hire expensive public relations firms to contain the damage.

Line G: Reputation costs _____

Total Cost of One Conflict

Add lines **C**, **D**, **E**, **F**, and **G** to determine the total estimated cost of this conflict.

Line H: Total cost of one conflict _____

Total Annual Cost of Conflict

While you may be shocked by the number on Line **H**, let's not forget that this is just one conflict. How many conflicts arise across the organization in a year? If you are part of a large, multinational enterprise, the answer could be thousands. Feel free to make a guess at that number on Line **I**.

Line I: Number of conflicts each year across the organization

Now, to find the number that may knock you out of your chair, multiply Line **H** by Line **I** (**H** x **I**) for an estimate of what your organization is spending on conflict each year.

Line J: Total annual cost of conflict

You're likely looking at a very large number—large enough to inspire you to do better at preventing and managing conflict. If you could reduce these conflict costs, how would you invest the savings in your mission or people?

Note: This worksheet is adapted from an activity in the *Have a Nice Conflict Learning Experience* by Tim Scudder and Michael Patterson, and used with the permission of Core Strengths, Inc.

acknowledgements

T HIS BOOK IS nearly 40 years in the making because it represents lessons learned over the course of my entire adult life. Some instruction, I eagerly embraced. Unfortunately, I also resisted important lessons that could have changed the trajectory of my career if I had been more open sooner. Looking back, I benefitted most from the lessons learned during tough times and difficult circumstances. But that's how life tends to work.

Over the years, my journey was enriched by highly effective leaders and wonderful colleagues. These men and women sharpened and shaped me, but always gave me a voice and opportunities to soar. I also learned a great deal from those who were less effective—even those who wreaked havoc and caused discomfort for many. These people are important, too, because the challenges they presented forced me to think, grow, and develop a resolve to do things differently when given the chance. So, to all of these men and women, I owe a tremendous debt of gratitude.

The "mission first, people always" mantra initially came to my attention as an Army ROTC cadet at Wheaton College and then as a young officer. Over those ten or so very formative years during which I proudly wore the Army's uniform on a daily basis, I learned so many great lessons about putting the interests of others above my own, respecting the wisdom of seasoned and sometimes crusty noncommissioned officers who knew more about getting things done in the face of adversity than I'll ever know, and how serving a cause far greater than oneself brings a sense of pride and fulfillment that extends beyond tangible rewards. I offer my special thanks to the late Lt. Col. Richard H. Dow, a Vietnam era warrior who demonstrated his belief in me with his time and mentorship. To all with whom I served and those who continue to serve, I salute you.

It's also important for me to recognize some key people who made this book in its present form possible. I am most grateful for the strategic guidance and practical suggestions so generously provided by Stephen Caldwell, a masterful writer. Stephen also introduced me to my editor, James Gilzow, who actively applied the harsh pen of a grizzled newspaperman to my work in order to make it much better. Both are proud sons of Arkansas and supremely good men. I am fortunate to know them.

More recently, I was greatly assisted by Jenna Reynolds. Jenna is an extremely talented graphic designer just getting started in her career, but I have no doubt that someday she will be famous and unaffordable. Her artistic vision made this a much more attractive product and her diligence with the details got us across the finish line.

I am also grateful to my good friend, Dr. Gil Brady, who so graciously agreed to write the foreword to the book. Gil embodies the ethos of mission first, people always, as he generously shares wisdom and unending kindness with so many people that cross his path.

His work as head of Nativity Prep Academy in San Diego changes lives every day.

Finally, my wife, Eunice, has served as my chief encourager throughout this project—and for the last 28 years. Beyond the book, she has tolerated my life on the road for too many years and deserved far more than she received at times. Fortunately, that's changed, and together we're going to continue to do great things for years to come.

Readers, thank you for your patronage. I wrote this book with hopes that you would benefit—even in some small way—so that you could achieve more and be better for the people who will make your success possible.

about the author

Dr. Mike Patterson is a consultant, educator, and speaker committed to helping leaders and teams achieve more by working better together. In addition to his work with clients, Mike teaches in the doctoral programs at Pepperdine University's Graduate School of Education and Psychology, as well as California Baptist University, and is a frequent conference and keynote speaker.

Mike began his career as a U.S. Army officer, and then served in a variety of commercial roles at TAP and Takeda Pharmaceuticals. More recently, he was a principal and thought leader at Core Strengths, the global talent development company and creator of the world's first digital platform to promote collaboration and improve communication. While at Core Strengths, Mike became a master facilitator of all learning based on the SDI 2.0, a valid and reliable assessment that helps people build their relationship intelligence (RQ).

His previous book, *Have a Nice Conflict: How to Find Success and Satisfaction in the Most Unlikely Places*, coauthored with Tim Scudder and Kent Mitchell, is a business fable loosely based on Mike's life and experiences. Widely acclaimed, "HANC" was the basis for a successful training program on conflict prevention and management.

Mike lives in the hills above Temecula, CA, with his beautiful wife, Eunice, where they enjoy hosting family and friends at their vineyard property.

Learn more about his work at www.drmikepatterson.com or contact him directly at mike@drmikepatterson.com.

Ambassador Associates is the consulting firm through which Dr. Mike Patterson and his associates serve clients. Whether it's team building, developing leadership across the enterprise, or designing a learning strategy to drive competitive advantage, Ambassador offers clients a broad spectrum of cost-effective talent development services. Based on an assessment of needs, Dr. Mike can tap into his network of subject matter experts, instructional designers, master facilitators, and coaches to design and deliver the most effective solution.

Over the last 15 years, Mike and his colleagues have worked with hundreds of clients from a wide array of organizations. From small nonprofits to Fortune 500 global giants, all need to drive results and develop people. Unfortunately, it's often the people issues that most interfere with performance and derail projects. That's Ambassador's specialty—bridging the people and performance gap. In fact, the name "Ambassador" is derived from our desire to bring people together and represent best practices in contemporary leadership.

Because Ambassador is small and not burdened by the cost structure of many larger training companies or consulting firms, we can work more cost effectively with clients and partner with them to achieve their desired results. No job is too small, and we can also scale up to meet the largest challenges. Please contact mike@drmikepatterson.com to learn more.